Plan
Reflect
Repeat

THE
WHITTAKER
JOURNAL

Plan
Reflect
Repeat

Thorsons

Thorsons
An imprint of HarperCollins*Publishers*
1 London Bridge Street
London SE1 9GF

www.harpercollins.co.uk

HarperCollins*Publishers*
Macken House, 39/40 Mayor Street Upper
Dublin 1, D01 C9W8, Ireland

First published by Thorsons 2023

1 3 5 7 9 10 8 6 4 2

Design by Catherine Wood © HarperCollins*Publishers*
Illustrations: Shutterstock.com

A catalogue record of this book is available from the British Library

ISBN 978-0-00-857980-7

Printed and bound by PNB, Latvia

This book is produced from independently certified FSC™ paper to ensure
responsible forest management.

For more information visit: www.harpercollins.co.uk/green

CONTENTS

Introduction

Hello and welcome to your *Plan, Reflect, Repeat* journal! I am
so excited that you are here and I'm so grateful to have had the
opportunity to create my idea of the ultimate life planner: *Plan,
Reflect, Repeat*. From planning as often and in as much detail as
you want, to reflecting and checking in on how you're feeling along
the way. I really feel this covers all the bases for feeling motivated,
organised and confident throughout life. Those three things are all
things that I have really struggled with in the past and over the years
I have had countless planners and mental health journals seperately,
to allow myself to not only plan and organise my life but also keep
on top of how I'm feeling along the way.

I searched high and low for a planner that ran the concepts of
planning and reflecting side by side but I never found one. When the
opportunity arose to create my very own dream planner/journal I
was so excited. I knew exactly what concept I wanted to create and I
had even had the title in my head for a long time before this became
a reality. I can't believe it's here! This concept has truly been life
changing for me and I hope it is for you too. Let's get started!

If today you
gave 10% but you
only had 10% to
give, then you
still gave 100%

How To Use This Planner

Ultimately, the best way to use this planner is in whatever way works best for you. The last thing I wanted to create was a planner that left you feeling unmotivated and uninspired. Essentially, this planner has three main uses.

Planning: for planning whatever you have coming up in your life whether it be events, work, school, weekends, holidays, appointments, time off, short term plans, long term plans, whatever you need! This can be done daily, weekly and monthly, and can be started and stopped whenever suits you.

Reflecting: for keeping in check with how you're feeling along the way. Even just acknowledging and processing how you're feeling is a huge step forward towards better mental health and in turn a happier, more motivated lifestyle. Again, just like the planning pages, reflecting can be done daily, weekly and monthly, and should be done however and whenever it suits you best.

Reflection: towards the back of the planner you'll find a section full of mindfulness activities from anxiety dumps to self-care day planners. These are all activities I have used and loved over the years and have really helped me process anxious thoughts, deal with stressful situations and care for myself more. They are to be used as and when you feel is best for you.

Seeing as my goal was to create the ultimate life planner, I wanted to have the option to plan daily, weekly and monthly all in one planner! As someone with dyslexia I find visualization is one of the only ways I can get organised and feel in control of my tasks for the day, week or month ahead. I hope this planner allows you to take life one day at a time by planning short term but also allowing you to see the bigger picture of your weeks and months throughout the year. Creating an organised visual plan at different stages (daily, weekly, monthly) has been the key to help keep me motivated throughout the year.

The amount of planning and reflecting you want to do will be a personal preference but will also change over time. This is is why I made sure not to use specific dates or months within the planner as sometimes it might suit you to plan loads for a few weeks and then take some down time and then pick it back up a few weeks later. Or, you might be like me and feel like you can't go a day without planning or getting your thoughts down on paper! I wanted to cater to a variety of planning and reflecting preferences, so I know you'll be able to find exactly what works best for you. Now let's run through some examples!

Monthly plan

I love being able to plan and see an overview of my month ahead. From important appointments to birthdays or holidays, I love seeing it all together in one big picture. You can plan your month in as much or as little detail as you like.

monthly plan

MONTH:

SUNDAY	MONDAY	TUESDAY	WEDNESDAY	THURSDAY

Did I make time for self-care this month?

I find it's so important to try to make time for a bit of self-care every month. It can be as simple as doing some journalling with a cup of tea, having a bubble bath or getting your nails done. Anything that is setting time for yourself, to care for yourself in whatever way feels good for you.

Things I found stressful this month
This section is for looking back on the month and processing what may have been hard for you. It might seem strange to focus on things that were hard but I've found it's such an amazing way to process your emotions properly and be able to move forward into next month feeling in control of your life.

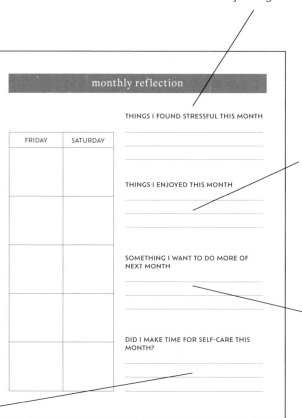

Things I enjoyed this month
Life moves so quickly and little or big moments that we enjoyed are so easily forgotten. I find that writing them down, no matter how little or insignificant they might seem, really helps me to reframe my view on the month and keep creating the positive energy I want for the month ahead.

Something I want to do more of next month
This section is for focusing on the month ahead and what you'd like to do more of. It doesn't always have to be big goals, it can be the little things too that you'd like to make time for.

Weekly plan

This section allows you to plan from Monday to Sunday each week, giving you a clear overview of the week ahead. I find this really helps me when it comes to that new week anxiety of wanting to start the week productively and fit everything in but not knowing where to start.

To-do list

I love having an overall to-do list when I'm planning my week, as I often have things I know need doing but I haven't necessarily allocated a day to-do them on yet. This allows me to still keep them in focus and within my weekly plan.

Goals

This section is for things you don't necessarily have to plan into this week but things that you'd like to try to aim to do.

How I have felt overall this week

This section is for taking a minute to process how this week has felt on the whole. It doesn't matter if it's positive or negative or any other kind of emotion. I have found that just acknowledging my emotions really helps me feel less overwhelmed and anxious and more in control of my life.

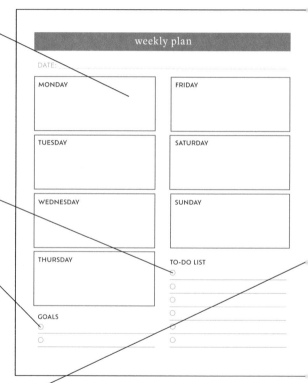

weekly plan

DATE:

MONDAY

TUESDAY

WEDNESDAY

THURSDAY

GOALS

FRIDAY

SATURDAY

SUNDAY

TO-DO LIST

What made me the happiest this week

This is for looking back at the end of your week and remembering what brought you joy. Life moves quickly and little weekly moments that have brought you happiness are so easily forgotten. I find that writing them down, no matter how little or insignificant they might seem, really helps me to keep creating the positive energy I want for the week ahead.

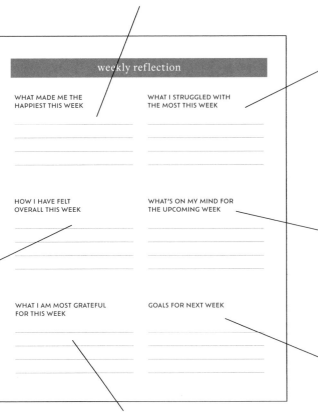

weekly reflection

WHAT MADE ME THE
HAPPIEST THIS WEEK

WHAT I STRUGGLED WITH
THE MOST THIS WEEK

HOW I HAVE FELT
OVERALL THIS WEEK

WHAT'S ON MY MIND FOR
THE UPCOMING WEEK

WHAT I AM MOST GRATEFUL
FOR THIS WEEK

GOALS FOR NEXT WEEK

What I struggled with the most this week

This is for looking back on the week and remembering what may have even difficult for you. It might seem strange to remember and focus on things that were hard during the week but it's a really amazing way to keep in check with your emotions, process them properly and be able to move forward into next week feeling in control.

What's on my mind for the upcoming week

This section allows you to process any emotions you might have about the upcoming week. I find this really helps me feel proactive about the week ahead

Goals for next week

This section allows you to think about any goals you might want to set yourself for the week ahead.

What I am most grateful for this week

As I said previously, gratitude is such a powerful emotion. I really find focusing on things that I'm grateful for, no matter how small, really creates the positive energy that I want to bring to each week.

Today's schedule

This section allows you to see the big picture of your whole day ahead from start to finish. This helps you feel less overwhelmed about the day ahead and more in control of what you want and need to get done.

Don't forget

Specific times of your appointments or events can get a bit lost within the overall plan of your day, so this section allows you to clearly see and remember those important times for your upcoming day.

Priorities

There are often times when you have a lot of things that you would like to plan into your day but not everything can realistically get done. Life happens and that's okay. This section allows you to single out the things that are your priority so you can keep them in focus throughout the day.

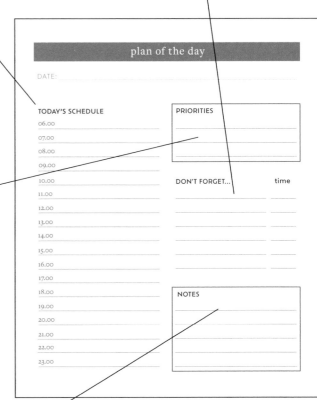

Notes

Use this section for whatever you need! You can jot down any extra information about your day, whether it's practical, like the address of an appointment, or more personal, like keeping track of how many glasses of water you've had, or even the weather forecast and what you plan to wear for an outing.

Something I found stressful today

This section allows you to think back on your day and process anything you found difficult or stressful. The days can go so quickly that we often forget to think about things we may have found hard, which for me can then turn into anxiety and feeling overwhelmed towards the end of the day.
Just taking a few minutes to acknowledge what I found stressful during the day, helps me process and control my emotions so much more positively.

Something I enjoyed today

Things you enjoyed during the day can so easily be forgotten about, as life moves so quickly. Taking time to reflect and remember those little enjoyable moments can really help re-frame your view of the day.

Something I am grateful for today

Gratitude is such a powerful emotion. Even on some of my worst days, thinking of one thing I'm grateful for can help my mindset and mood so much.

reflection

SOMETHING I FOUND STRESSFUL TODAY

SOMETHING I ENJOYED TODAY

SOMETHING I AM GRATEFUL FOR TODAY

HOW I'M FEELING ABOUT TOMORROW

How I'm feeling about tomorrow

This section allows you to think forward and process any emotions you may be feeling about the next day. Just taking time to acknowledge how you feel is an amazing first step to feeling more in control of your days.

PART ONE

Be the energy you
want to attract

Monthly Planner Introduction

In each section of planning whether it be the monthly, weekly or daily section, I wanted to have an option to plan but also reflect at each stage. Monthly planning is amazing for giving you the bigger picture of your month ahead before planning your weeks and days in more depth as they come around.

I also find it really helpful and motivating to reflect at the end of each month on how I've been feeling. Whether it's been a great month or a really hard month, I found it really helps when preparing to go into the next month as motivated and content as you can be, to look back, debrief and acknowledge your emotions.

monthly plan

MONTH: ....

SUNDAY	MONDAY	TUESDAY	WEDNESDAY	THURSDAY

monthly reflection

FRIDAY	SATURDAY

THINGS I FOUND STRESSFUL THIS MONTH

_____

_____

_____

THINGS I ENJOYED THIS MONTH

_____

_____

_____

SOMETHING I WANT TO DO MORE OF
NEXT MONTH

_____

_____

_____

DID I MAKE TIME FOR SELF-CARE THIS
MONTH?

_____

_____

_____

monthly plan

MONTH: ....

SUNDAY	MONDAY	TUESDAY	WEDNESDAY	THURSDAY

FRIDAY	SATURDAY

THINGS I FOUND STRESSFUL THIS MONTH

THINGS I ENJOYED THIS MONTH

SOMETHING I WANT TO DO MORE OF
NEXT MONTH

DID I MAKE TIME FOR SELF-CARE THIS
MONTH?

monthly plan

MONTH: ....

SUNDAY	MONDAY	TUESDAY	WEDNESDAY	THURSDAY

monthly reflection

FRIDAY	SATURDAY

THINGS I FOUND STRESSFUL THIS MONTH

_____

_____

_____

THINGS I ENJOYED THIS MONTH

_____

_____

_____

SOMETHING I WANT TO DO MORE OF
NEXT MONTH

_____

_____

_____

DID I MAKE TIME FOR SELF-CARE THIS
MONTH?

_____

_____

_____

Don't compare
yourself to others.
There's no comparison
between the sun and
the moon, they shine
when it's their time

Weekly Planner Introduction

Weekly planning is one of my favourite types of planning because I'm someone who tends to get overwhelmed at the start of the week with the pressure to 'smash this week' and achieve all my goals. Then by about Thursday I've totally lost motviation and I'm ready to sit on the sofa in my PJs until the next week starts. I have really found that weekly planning allows me to understand and process what the next week entails and feel organised and in control going into it. As the week goes on it helps me to visually see how much I've already done and what I've got left to keep me motivated as I work towards the weekend!

After each weekly planning page we then have weekly reflections, which I have found so helpful when processing how my week has been. Sometimes a week can fly by so fast you can barely remember what you did and how you felt. Especially if your week ends in a struggle or with a difficult or stressful situation, it can leave you feeling so negative as you go into the weekend or the week ahead. Actually taking time to process the good and bad parts of each week has been a game changer and has made me feel so much more present in my life and at peace with the range of emotions that come with each week.

weekly plan

MONDAY

FRIDAY

TUESDAY

SATURDAY

WEDNESDAY

SUNDAY

THURSDAY

TO-DO LIST
- ○
- ○
- ○
- ○
- ○
- ○

GOALS
- ○
- ○

weekly reflection

WHAT MADE ME THE
HAPPIEST THIS WEEK

_____

_____

_____

_____

WHAT I STRUGGLED WITH
THE MOST THIS WEEK

_____

_____

_____

_____

HOW I HAVE FELT
OVERALL THIS WEEK

_____

_____

_____

_____

WHAT'S ON MY MIND FOR
THE UPCOMING WEEK

_____

_____

_____

_____

WHAT I AM MOST GRATEFUL
FOR THIS WEEK

_____

_____

_____

_____

GOALS FOR NEXT WEEK

_____

_____

_____

_____

weekly plan

DATE:

MONDAY

FRIDAY

TUESDAY

SATURDAY

WEDNESDAY

SUNDAY

THURSDAY

TO-DO LIST

- ○
- ○
- ○
- ○
- ○
- ○

GOALS

- ○
- ○

weekly reflection

WHAT MADE ME THE
HAPPIEST THIS WEEK

_____

_____

_____

_____

WHAT I STRUGGLED WITH
THE MOST THIS WEEK

_____

_____

_____

_____

HOW I HAVE FELT
OVERALL THIS WEEK

_____

_____

_____

_____

WHAT'S ON MY MIND FOR
THE UPCOMING WEEK

_____

_____

_____

_____

WHAT I AM MOST GRATEFUL
FOR THIS WEEK

_____

_____

_____

_____

GOALS FOR NEXT WEEK

_____

_____

_____

_____

weekly plan

DATE: ....

MONDAY	FRIDAY

TUESDAY	SATURDAY

WEDNESDAY	SUNDAY

THURSDAY

GOALS
○ _____
○ _____

TO-DO LIST
○ _____
○ _____
○ _____
○ _____
○ _____
○ _____

weekly reflection

WHAT MADE ME THE
HAPPIEST THIS WEEK

_____

_____

_____

_____

WHAT I STRUGGLED WITH
THE MOST THIS WEEK

_____

_____

_____

_____

HOW I HAVE FELT
OVERALL THIS WEEK

_____

_____

_____

_____

WHAT'S ON MY MIND FOR
THE UPCOMING WEEK

_____

_____

_____

_____

WHAT I AM MOST GRATEFUL
FOR THIS WEEK

_____

_____

_____

_____

GOALS FOR NEXT WEEK

_____

_____

_____

_____

weekly plan

DATE: ....

MONDAY

TUESDAY

WEDNESDAY

THURSDAY

GOALS
○ _____
○ _____

FRIDAY

SATURDAY

SUNDAY

TO-DO LIST
○ _____
○ _____
○ _____
○ _____
○ _____
○ _____

weekly reflection

WHAT MADE ME THE
HAPPIEST THIS WEEK

_____

_____

_____

_____

WHAT I STRUGGLED WITH
THE MOST THIS WEEK

_____

_____

_____

_____

HOW I HAVE FELT
OVERALL THIS WEEK

_____

_____

_____

_____

WHAT'S ON MY MIND FOR
THE UPCOMING WEEK

_____

_____

_____

_____

WHAT I AM MOST GRATEFUL
FOR THIS WEEK

_____

_____

_____

_____

GOALS FOR NEXT WEEK

_____

_____

_____

_____

weekly plan

DATE: ....

MONDAY

FRIDAY

TUESDAY

SATURDAY

WEDNESDAY

SUNDAY

THURSDAY

GOALS
○ _____
○ _____

TO-DO LIST
○ _____
○ _____
○ _____
○ _____
○ _____
○ _____

weekly reflection

WHAT MADE ME THE HAPPIEST THIS WEEK

_____
_____
_____
_____

WHAT I STRUGGLED WITH THE MOST THIS WEEK

_____
_____
_____
_____

HOW I HAVE FELT OVERALL THIS WEEK

_____
_____
_____
_____

WHAT'S ON MY MIND FOR THE UPCOMING WEEK

_____
_____
_____
_____

WHAT I AM MOST GRATEFUL FOR THIS WEEK

_____
_____
_____
_____

GOALS FOR NEXT WEEK

_____
_____
_____
_____

weekly plan

DATE: ....

MONDAY

FRIDAY

TUESDAY

SATURDAY

WEDNESDAY

SUNDAY

THURSDAY

TO-DO LIST
- ○ _____
- ○ _____
- ○ _____
- ○ _____
- ○ _____
- ○ _____

GOALS
- ○ _____
- ○ _____

weekly reflection

WHAT MADE ME THE
HAPPIEST THIS WEEK

_____
_____
_____
_____

WHAT I STRUGGLED WITH
THE MOST THIS WEEK

_____
_____
_____
_____

HOW I HAVE FELT
OVERALL THIS WEEK

_____
_____
_____
_____

WHAT'S ON MY MIND FOR
THE UPCOMING WEEK

_____
_____
_____
_____

WHAT I AM MOST GRATEFUL
FOR THIS WEEK

_____
_____
_____
_____

GOALS FOR NEXT WEEK

_____
_____
_____
_____

weekly plan

DATE: ....

MONDAY	FRIDAY

TUESDAY	SATURDAY

WEDNESDAY	SUNDAY

THURSDAY

GOALS
- ○ _____
- ○ _____

TO-DO LIST
- ○ _____
- ○ _____
- ○ _____
- ○ _____
- ○ _____
- ○ _____

weekly reflection

WHAT MADE ME THE
HAPPIEST THIS WEEK

_____

_____

_____

_____

WHAT I STRUGGLED WITH
THE MOST THIS WEEK

_____

_____

_____

_____

HOW I HAVE FELT
OVERALL THIS WEEK

_____

_____

_____

_____

WHAT'S ON MY MIND FOR
THE UPCOMING WEEK

_____

_____

_____

_____

WHAT I AM MOST GRATEFUL
FOR THIS WEEK

_____

_____

_____

_____

_____

GOALS FOR NEXT WEEK

_____

_____

_____

_____

_____

weekly plan

DATE: ....

MONDAY

TUESDAY

WEDNESDAY

THURSDAY

GOALS
- ○ ....
- ○ ....

FRIDAY

SATURDAY

SUNDAY

TO-DO LIST
- ○ ....
- ○ ....
- ○ ....
- ○ ....
- ○ ....
- ○ ....

weekly reflection

**WHAT MADE ME THE
HAPPIEST THIS WEEK**

_____

_____

_____

_____

**WHAT I STRUGGLED WITH
THE MOST THIS WEEK**

_____

_____

_____

_____

**HOW I HAVE FELT
OVERALL THIS WEEK**

_____

_____

_____

_____

**WHAT'S ON MY MIND FOR
THE UPCOMING WEEK**

_____

_____

_____

_____

**WHAT I AM MOST GRATEFUL
FOR THIS WEEK**

_____

_____

_____

_____

GOALS FOR NEXT WEEK

_____

_____

_____

_____

weekly plan

DATE: ....

MONDAY

TUESDAY

WEDNESDAY

THURSDAY

GOALS

○ _____

○ _____

FRIDAY

SATURDAY

SUNDAY

TO-DO LIST

○ _____

○ _____

○ _____

○ _____

○ _____

○ _____

weekly reflection

WHAT MADE ME THE
HAPPIEST THIS WEEK

_____

_____

_____

_____

WHAT I STRUGGLED WITH
THE MOST THIS WEEK

_____

_____

_____

_____

HOW I HAVE FELT
OVERALL THIS WEEK

_____

_____

_____

_____

WHAT'S ON MY MIND FOR
THE UPCOMING WEEK

_____

_____

_____

_____

WHAT I AM MOST GRATEFUL
FOR THIS WEEK

_____

_____

_____

_____

GOALS FOR NEXT WEEK

_____

_____

_____

_____

DATE: ....

MONDAY	FRIDAY

TUESDAY	SATURDAY

WEDNESDAY	SUNDAY

THURSDAY	

TO-DO LIST
- ◯
- ◯
- ◯
- ◯
- ◯
- ◯

GOALS
- ◯
- ◯

weekly reflection

WHAT MADE ME THE
HAPPIEST THIS WEEK

_____

_____

_____

_____

WHAT I STRUGGLED WITH
THE MOST THIS WEEK

_____

_____

_____

_____

HOW I HAVE FELT
OVERALL THIS WEEK

_____

_____

_____

_____

WHAT'S ON MY MIND FOR
THE UPCOMING WEEK

_____

_____

_____

_____

WHAT I AM MOST GRATEFUL
FOR THIS WEEK

_____

_____

_____

_____

GOALS FOR NEXT WEEK

_____

_____

_____

_____

DATE: ....

MONDAY	FRIDAY

TUESDAY	SATURDAY

WEDNESDAY	SUNDAY

THURSDAY

TO-DO LIST
- ○ _____
- ○ _____
- ○ _____
- ○ _____
- ○ _____
- ○ _____

GOALS
- ○ _____
- ○ _____

weekly reflection

WHAT MADE ME THE
HAPPIEST THIS WEEK

_____

_____

_____

_____

WHAT I STRUGGLED WITH
THE MOST THIS WEEK

_____

_____

_____

_____

HOW I HAVE FELT
OVERALL THIS WEEK

_____

_____

_____

_____

WHAT'S ON MY MIND FOR
THE UPCOMING WEEK

_____

_____

_____

_____

WHAT I AM MOST GRATEFUL
FOR THIS WEEK

_____

_____

_____

_____

_____

GOALS FOR NEXT WEEK

_____

_____

_____

_____

_____

weekly plan

DATE: ....

MONDAY	FRIDAY

TUESDAY	SATURDAY

WEDNESDAY	SUNDAY

THURSDAY

TO-DO LIST
- ○ _____
- ○ _____
- ○ _____
- ○ _____
- ○ _____
- ○ _____

GOALS
- ○ _____
- ○ _____

weekly reflection

**WHAT MADE ME THE
HAPPIEST THIS WEEK**

_____

_____

_____

_____

**WHAT I STRUGGLED WITH
THE MOST THIS WEEK**

_____

_____

_____

_____

**HOW I HAVE FELT
OVERALL THIS WEEK**

_____

_____

_____

_____

**WHAT'S ON MY MIND FOR
THE UPCOMING WEEK**

_____

_____

_____

_____

**WHAT I AM MOST GRATEFUL
FOR THIS WEEK**

_____

_____

_____

_____

GOALS FOR NEXT WEEK

_____

_____

_____

_____

Focus on the
step in front
of you, not the
whole staircase

Daily Planner Introduction

I have found that daily planning is absolutely key to keeping myself motivated throughout the day and stopping myself feeling too overwhelmed with juggling to-do lists, daunting appointments and social events. You can plan your day in as much or as little detail as suits you, from planning what each hour of the day could look like, to brief notes here and there to keep you on track.

After every daily planner there is an option to reflect. Just as a reminder, these sections are here to be used as frequently as you like and in a way that works for you. That might change as the weeks and months go by but having an option for daily reflecting has been really important to me – during particularly stressful or busy times in my life I have found a quick, simple daily reflection before bed has been life changing. It helps me really quickly process what's on my mind and what's running through my head, allowing me to feel in control of my thoughts and at peace with my emotions. Ready to take on the next day, whatever it may bring.

plan of the day

DATE: 30/08/23

TODAY'S SCHEDULE

06.00
07.00
08.00
09.00 Get up + dressed
10.00 Breakfast
11.00 Tidy kitchen
12.00 Washing
13.00 Lunch + make dinner
14.00 Walk
15.00 Hoover + mop
16.00 Jules' nap.
17.00 Sort Jules' wardrobe
18.00 Dinner
19.00
20.00
21.00
22.00
23.00

PRIORITIES

DON'T FORGET...   time

NOTES

reflection

SOMETHING I FOUND
STRESSFUL TODAY

SOMETHING I
ENJOYED TODAY

SOMETHING I AM GRATEFUL FOR TODAY

HOW I'M FEELING ABOUT TOMORROW

plan of the day

DATE: ....

TODAY'S SCHEDULE

06.00 _____

07.00 _____

08.00 _____

09.00 _____

10.00 _____

11.00 _____

12.00 _____

13.00 _____

14.00 _____

15.00 _____

16.00 _____

17.00 _____

18.00 _____

19.00 _____

20.00 _____

21.00 _____

22.00 _____

23.00 _____

PRIORITIES

DON'T FORGET...   time

NOTES

reflection

SOMETHING I FOUND STRESSFUL TODAY	SOMETHING I ENJOYED TODAY

SOMETHING I AM GRATEFUL FOR TODAY

HOW I'M FEELING ABOUT TOMORROW

plan of the day

DATE: ....

TODAY'S SCHEDULE

06.00 _____

07.00 _____

08.00 _____

09.00 _____

10.00 _____

11.00 _____

12.00 _____

13.00 _____

14.00 _____

15.00 _____

16.00 _____

17.00 _____

18.00 _____

19.00 _____

20.00 _____

21.00 _____

22.00 _____

23.00 _____

PRIORITIES

DON'T FORGET...   time

NOTES

reflection

SOMETHING I FOUND
STRESSFUL TODAY

SOMETHING I
ENJOYED TODAY

SOMETHING I AM GRATEFUL FOR TODAY

HOW I'M FEELING ABOUT TOMORROW

plan of the day

DATE: ....

TODAY'S SCHEDULE

06.00
07.00
08.00
09.00
10.00
11.00
12.00
13.00
14.00
15.00
16.00
17.00
18.00
19.00
20.00
21.00
22.00
23.00

PRIORITIES

DON'T FORGET...   time

NOTES

reflection

SOMETHING I FOUND
STRESSFUL TODAY

SOMETHING I
ENJOYED TODAY

SOMETHING I AM GRATEFUL FOR TODAY

HOW I'M FEELING ABOUT TOMORROW

plan of the day

DATE: ....

TODAY'S SCHEDULE

06.00

07.00

08.00

09.00

10.00

11.00

12.00

13.00

14.00

15.00

16.00

17.00

18.00

19.00

20.00

21.00

22.00

23.00

PRIORITIES

DON'T FORGET...   time

NOTES

reflection

SOMETHING I FOUND STRESSFUL TODAY

SOMETHING I ENJOYED TODAY

SOMETHING I AM GRATEFUL FOR TODAY

HOW I'M FEELING ABOUT TOMORROW

plan of the day

DATE: ....

TODAY'S SCHEDULE

06.00
07.00
08.00
09.00
10.00
11.00
12.00
13.00
14.00
15.00
16.00
17.00
18.00
19.00
20.00
21.00
22.00
23.00

PRIORITIES

DON'T FORGET...   time

NOTES

reflection

SOMETHING I FOUND STRESSFUL TODAY	SOMETHING I ENJOYED TODAY

SOMETHING I AM GRATEFUL FOR TODAY

HOW I'M FEELING ABOUT TOMORROW

plan of the day

DATE: ....

TODAY'S SCHEDULE

06.00
07.00
08.00
09.00
10.00
11.00
12.00
13.00
14.00
15.00
16.00
17.00
18.00
19.00
20.00
21.00
22.00
23.00

PRIORITIES

DON'T FORGET...   time

NOTES

reflection

SOMETHING I FOUND STRESSFUL TODAY	SOMETHING I ENJOYED TODAY

SOMETHING I AM GRATEFUL FOR TODAY

HOW I'M FEELING ABOUT TOMORROW

plan of the day

DATE: ....

TODAY'S SCHEDULE

06.00 _____

07.00 _____

08.00 _____

09.00 _____

10.00 _____

11.00 _____

12.00 _____

13.00 _____

14.00 _____

15.00 _____

16.00 _____

17.00 _____

18.00 _____

19.00 _____

20.00 _____

21.00 _____

22.00 _____

23.00 _____

PRIORITIES

_____

_____

_____

DON'T FORGET...   time

_____ _____

_____ _____

_____ _____

_____ _____

_____ _____

_____ _____

NOTES

_____

_____

_____

_____

_____

reflection

SOMETHING I FOUND STRESSFUL TODAY	SOMETHING I ENJOYED TODAY

SOMETHING I AM GRATEFUL FOR TODAY

HOW I'M FEELING ABOUT TOMORROW

plan of the day

DATE: ....

TODAY'S SCHEDULE

06.00 _____

07.00 _____

08.00 _____

09.00 _____

10.00 _____

11.00 _____

12.00 _____

13.00 _____

14.00 _____

15.00 _____

16.00 _____

17.00 _____

18.00 _____

19.00 _____

20.00 _____

21.00 _____

22.00 _____

23.00 _____

PRIORITIES

_____

_____

_____

DON'T FORGET...   time

_____ ____

_____ ____

_____ ____

_____ ____

_____ ____

_____ ____

NOTES

_____

_____

_____

_____

_____

reflection

SOMETHING I FOUND
STRESSFUL TODAY

SOMETHING I
ENJOYED TODAY

SOMETHING I AM GRATEFUL FOR TODAY

HOW I'M FEELING ABOUT TOMORROW

plan of the day

DATE: ....

TODAY'S SCHEDULE

06.00

07.00

08.00

09.00

10.00

11.00

12.00

13.00

14.00

15.00

16.00

17.00

18.00

19.00

20.00

21.00

22.00

23.00

PRIORITIES

DON'T FORGET...   time

NOTES

reflection

SOMETHING I FOUND
STRESSFUL TODAY

SOMETHING I
ENJOYED TODAY

SOMETHING I AM GRATEFUL FOR TODAY

HOW I'M FEELING ABOUT TOMORROW

plan of the day

DATE: ....

TODAY'S SCHEDULE

06.00

07.00

08.00

09.00

10.00

11.00

12.00

13.00

14.00

15.00

16.00

17.00

18.00

19.00

20.00

21.00

22.00

23.00

PRIORITIES

DON'T FORGET...   time

NOTES

reflection

SOMETHING I FOUND
STRESSFUL TODAY

SOMETHING I
ENJOYED TODAY

SOMETHING I AM GRATEFUL FOR TODAY

HOW I'M FEELING ABOUT TOMORROW

plan of the day

DATE: ....

TODAY'S SCHEDULE

06.00

07.00

08.00

09.00

10.00

11.00

12.00

13.00

14.00

15.00

16.00

17.00

18.00

19.00

20.00

21.00

22.00

23.00

PRIORITIES

DON'T FORGET...   time

NOTES

reflection

SOMETHING I FOUND
STRESSFUL TODAY

SOMETHING I
ENJOYED TODAY

SOMETHING I AM GRATEFUL FOR TODAY

HOW I'M FEELING ABOUT TOMORROW

plan of the day

DATE: ....

TODAY'S SCHEDULE

06.00
07.00
08.00
09.00
10.00
11.00
12.00
13.00
14.00
15.00
16.00
17.00
18.00
19.00
20.00
21.00
22.00
23.00

PRIORITIES

DON'T FORGET...   time

NOTES

reflection

SOMETHING I FOUND STRESSFUL TODAY

_____

_____

_____

_____

_____

_____

_____

SOMETHING I ENJOYED TODAY

_____

_____

_____

_____

_____

_____

_____

SOMETHING I AM GRATEFUL FOR TODAY

_____

_____

_____

_____

HOW I'M FEELING ABOUT TOMORROW

_____

_____

_____

_____

plan of the day

DATE: ....

TODAY'S SCHEDULE

06.00

07.00

08.00

09.00

10.00

11.00

12.00

13.00

14.00

15.00

16.00

17.00

18.00

19.00

20.00

21.00

22.00

23.00

PRIORITIES

DON'T FORGET...   time

NOTES

reflection

SOMETHING I FOUND
STRESSFUL TODAY

SOMETHING I
ENJOYED TODAY

SOMETHING I AM GRATEFUL FOR TODAY

HOW I'M FEELING ABOUT TOMORROW

plan of the day

DATE: ....

TODAY'S SCHEDULE

06.00 _____

07.00 _____

08.00 _____

09.00 _____

10.00 _____

11.00 _____

12.00 _____

13.00 _____

14.00 _____

15.00 _____

16.00 _____

17.00 _____

18.00 _____

19.00 _____

20.00 _____

21.00 _____

22.00 _____

23.00 _____

PRIORITIES

_____

_____

_____

DON'T FORGET...   time

_____ _____

_____ _____

_____ _____

_____ _____

_____ _____

_____ _____

NOTES

_____

_____

_____

_____

_____

reflection

**SOMETHING I FOUND
STRESSFUL TODAY**

**SOMETHING I
ENJOYED TODAY**

SOMETHING I AM GRATEFUL FOR TODAY

HOW I'M FEELING ABOUT TOMORROW

plan of the day

DATE: ....

TODAY'S SCHEDULE

06.00

07.00

08.00

09.00

10.00

11.00

12.00

13.00

14.00

15.00

16.00

17.00

18.00

19.00

20.00

21.00

22.00

23.00

PRIORITIES

DON'T FORGET...   time

NOTES

reflection

SOMETHING I FOUND
STRESSFUL TODAY

SOMETHING I
ENJOYED TODAY

SOMETHING I AM GRATEFUL FOR TODAY

HOW I'M FEELING ABOUT TOMORROW

plan of the day

DATE: ....

TODAY'S SCHEDULE

06.00 _____

07.00 _____

08.00 _____

09.00 _____

10.00 _____

11.00 _____

12.00 _____

13.00 _____

14.00 _____

15.00 _____

16.00 _____

17.00 _____

18.00 _____

19.00 _____

20.00 _____

21.00 _____

22.00 _____

23.00 _____

PRIORITIES

DON'T FORGET...   time

NOTES

reflection

SOMETHING I FOUND STRESSFUL TODAY

SOMETHING I ENJOYED TODAY

SOMETHING I AM GRATEFUL FOR TODAY

HOW I'M FEELING ABOUT TOMORROW

plan of the day

DATE: ....

TODAY'S SCHEDULE

06.00

07.00

08.00

09.00

10.00

11.00

12.00

13.00

14.00

15.00

16.00

17.00

18.00

19.00

20.00

21.00

22.00

23.00

PRIORITIES

DON'T FORGET...   time

NOTES

reflection

SOMETHING I FOUND STRESSFUL TODAY

_____
_____
_____
_____
_____
_____
_____

SOMETHING I ENJOYED TODAY

_____
_____
_____
_____
_____
_____
_____

SOMETHING I AM GRATEFUL FOR TODAY

_____
_____
_____
_____

HOW I'M FEELING ABOUT TOMORROW

_____
_____
_____
_____

plan of the day

DATE: ....

TODAY'S SCHEDULE

06.00

07.00

08.00

09.00

10.00

11.00

12.00

13.00

14.00

15.00

16.00

17.00

18.00

19.00

20.00

21.00

22.00

23.00

PRIORITIES

DON'T FORGET...   time

NOTES

reflection

SOMETHING I FOUND
STRESSFUL TODAY

SOMETHING I
ENJOYED TODAY

SOMETHING I AM GRATEFUL FOR TODAY

HOW I'M FEELING ABOUT TOMORROW

plan of the day

DATE: ....

TODAY'S SCHEDULE

06.00 _____

07.00 _____

08.00 _____

09.00 _____

10.00 _____

11.00 _____

12.00 _____

13.00 _____

14.00 _____

15.00 _____

16.00 _____

17.00 _____

18.00 _____

19.00 _____

20.00 _____

21.00 _____

22.00 _____

23.00 _____

PRIORITIES

_____

_____

_____

DON'T FORGET...   time

_____ _____

_____ _____

_____ _____

_____ _____

_____ _____

NOTES

_____

_____

_____

_____

_____

reflection

SOMETHING I FOUND
STRESSFUL TODAY

SOMETHING I
ENJOYED TODAY

SOMETHING I AM GRATEFUL FOR TODAY

HOW I'M FEELING ABOUT TOMORROW

plan of the day

DATE: ....

TODAY'S SCHEDULE

06.00

07.00

08.00

09.00

10.00

11.00

12.00

13.00

14.00

15.00

16.00

17.00

18.00

19.00

20.00

21.00

22.00

23.00

PRIORITIES

DON'T FORGET...   time

NOTES

reflection

SOMETHING I FOUND
STRESSFUL TODAY

_____

_____

_____

_____

_____

_____

_____

SOMETHING I
ENJOYED TODAY

_____

_____

_____

_____

_____

_____

_____

SOMETHING I AM GRATEFUL FOR TODAY

_____

_____

_____

_____

HOW I'M FEELING ABOUT TOMORROW

_____

_____

_____

_____

plan of the day

DATE: ....

TODAY'S SCHEDULE

06.00 _____

07.00 _____

08.00 _____

09.00 _____

10.00 _____

11.00 _____

12.00 _____

13.00 _____

14.00 _____

15.00 _____

16.00 _____

17.00 _____

18.00 _____

19.00 _____

20.00 _____

21.00 _____

22.00 _____

23.00 _____

PRIORITIES

_____

_____

_____

DON'T FORGET...   time

_____ _____

_____ _____

_____ _____

_____ _____

_____ _____

_____ _____

NOTES

_____

_____

_____

_____

_____

_____

reflection

SOMETHING I FOUND STRESSFUL TODAY

SOMETHING I ENJOYED TODAY

SOMETHING I AM GRATEFUL FOR TODAY

HOW I'M FEELING ABOUT TOMORROW

plan of the day

DATE: ....

TODAY'S SCHEDULE

06.00 _____
07.00 _____
08.00 _____
09.00 _____
10.00 _____
11.00 _____
12.00 _____
13.00 _____
14.00 _____
15.00 _____
16.00 _____
17.00 _____
18.00 _____
19.00 _____
20.00 _____
21.00 _____
22.00 _____
23.00 _____

PRIORITIES

_____
_____
_____

DON'T FORGET...   time

_____ _____
_____ _____
_____ _____
_____ _____
_____ _____
_____ _____

NOTES

_____
_____
_____
_____
_____

reflection

SOMETHING I FOUND STRESSFUL TODAY

_____
_____
_____
_____
_____
_____
_____

SOMETHING I ENJOYED TODAY

_____
_____
_____
_____
_____
_____
_____

SOMETHING I AM GRATEFUL FOR TODAY

_____
_____
_____
_____

HOW I'M FEELING ABOUT TOMORROW

_____
_____
_____
_____

DATE: ....

TODAY'S SCHEDULE

06.00 _____

07.00 _____

08.00 _____

09.00 _____

10.00 _____

11.00 _____

12.00 _____

13.00 _____

14.00 _____

15.00 _____

16.00 _____

17.00 _____

18.00 _____

19.00 _____

20.00 _____

21.00 _____

22.00 _____

23.00 _____

PRIORITIES

_____

_____

_____

DON'T FORGET...   time

_____ _____

_____ _____

_____ _____

_____ _____

_____ _____

_____ _____

NOTES

_____

_____

_____

_____

_____

_____

reflection

SOMETHING I FOUND STRESSFUL TODAY	SOMETHING I ENJOYED TODAY

SOMETHING I AM GRATEFUL FOR TODAY

HOW I'M FEELING ABOUT TOMORROW

plan of the day

DATE: ....

TODAY'S SCHEDULE

06.00 _____

07.00 _____

08.00 _____

09.00 _____

10.00 _____

11.00 _____

12.00 _____

13.00 _____

14.00 _____

15.00 _____

16.00 _____

17.00 _____

18.00 _____

19.00 _____

20.00 _____

21.00 _____

22.00 _____

23.00 _____

PRIORITIES

_____

_____

_____

DON'T FORGET...   time

_____   _____

_____   _____

_____   _____

_____   _____

_____   _____

_____   _____

NOTES

_____

_____

_____

_____

_____

_____

reflection

SOMETHING I FOUND
STRESSFUL TODAY

SOMETHING I
ENJOYED TODAY

SOMETHING I AM GRATEFUL FOR TODAY

HOW I'M FEELING ABOUT TOMORROW

plan of the day

DATE: ....

TODAY'S SCHEDULE

06.00

07.00

08.00

09.00

10.00

11.00

12.00

13.00

14.00

15.00

16.00

17.00

18.00

19.00

20.00

21.00

22.00

23.00

PRIORITIES

DON'T FORGET...   time

NOTES

reflection

SOMETHING I FOUND STRESSFUL TODAY

_____

_____

_____

_____

_____

_____

_____

SOMETHING I ENJOYED TODAY

_____

_____

_____

_____

_____

_____

_____

SOMETHING I AM GRATEFUL FOR TODAY

_____

_____

_____

_____

HOW I'M FEELING ABOUT TOMORROW

_____

_____

_____

_____

plan of the day

DATE: ....

TODAY'S SCHEDULE

06.00
07.00
08.00
09.00
10.00
11.00
12.00
13.00
14.00
15.00
16.00
17.00
18.00
19.00
20.00
21.00
22.00
23.00

PRIORITIES

DON'T FORGET...   time

NOTES

reflection

SOMETHING I FOUND
STRESSFUL TODAY

_____

_____

_____

_____

_____

_____

SOMETHING I
ENJOYED TODAY

_____

_____

_____

_____

_____

_____

SOMETHING I AM GRATEFUL FOR TODAY

_____

_____

_____

HOW I'M FEELING ABOUT TOMORROW

_____

_____

_____

_____

plan of the day

DATE: ....

TODAY'S SCHEDULE

06.00

07.00

08.00

09.00

10.00

11.00

12.00

13.00

14.00

15.00

16.00

17.00

18.00

19.00

20.00

21.00

22.00

23.00

PRIORITIES

DON'T FORGET...   time

NOTES

reflection

SOMETHING I FOUND
STRESSFUL TODAY

SOMETHING I
ENJOYED TODAY

SOMETHING I AM GRATEFUL FOR TODAY

HOW I'M FEELING ABOUT TOMORROW

plan of the day

DATE: ....

TODAY'S SCHEDULE

06.00

07.00

08.00

09.00

10.00

11.00

12.00

13.00

14.00

15.00

16.00

17.00

18.00

19.00

20.00

21.00

22.00

23.00

PRIORITIES

DON'T FORGET...   time

NOTES

reflection

**SOMETHING I FOUND
STRESSFUL TODAY**

_____

_____

_____

_____

_____

_____

_____

**SOMETHING I
ENJOYED TODAY**

_____

_____

_____

_____

_____

_____

_____

SOMETHING I AM GRATEFUL FOR TODAY

_____

_____

_____

_____

HOW I'M FEELING ABOUT TOMORROW

_____

_____

_____

_____

plan of the day

DATE: ....

TODAY'S SCHEDULE

06.00 _____

07.00 _____

08.00 _____

09.00 _____

10.00 _____

11.00 _____

12.00 _____

13.00 _____

14.00 _____

15.00 _____

16.00 _____

17.00 _____

18.00 _____

19.00 _____

20.00 _____

21.00 _____

22.00 _____

23.00 _____

PRIORITIES

_____

_____

_____

DON'T FORGET...   time

_____   _____

_____   _____

_____   _____

_____   _____

_____   _____

_____   _____

NOTES

_____

_____

_____

_____

_____

_____

reflection

SOMETHING I FOUND STRESSFUL TODAY

_____

_____

_____

_____

_____

_____

_____

SOMETHING I ENJOYED TODAY

_____

_____

_____

_____

_____

_____

_____

SOMETHING I AM GRATEFUL FOR TODAY

_____

_____

_____

_____

HOW I'M FEELING ABOUT TOMORROW

_____

_____

_____

_____

plan of the day

DATE: ....

TODAY'S SCHEDULE

06.00

07.00

08.00

09.00

10.00

11.00

12.00

13.00

14.00

15.00

16.00

17.00

18.00

19.00

20.00

21.00

22.00

23.00

PRIORITIES

DON'T FORGET...   time

NOTES

reflection

SOMETHING I FOUND STRESSFUL TODAY	SOMETHING I ENJOYED TODAY

SOMETHING I AM GRATEFUL FOR TODAY

HOW I'M FEELING ABOUT TOMORROW

plan of the day

DATE: ....

TODAY'S SCHEDULE

06.00 _____

07.00 _____

08.00 _____

09.00 _____

10.00 _____

11.00 _____

12.00 _____

13.00 _____

14.00 _____

15.00 _____

16.00 _____

17.00 _____

18.00 _____

19.00 _____

20.00 _____

21.00 _____

22.00 _____

23.00 _____

PRIORITIES

_____

_____

_____

DON'T FORGET...   time

_____   _____

_____   _____

_____   _____

_____   _____

_____   _____

_____   _____

NOTES

_____

_____

_____

_____

_____

reflection

SOMETHING I FOUND STRESSFUL TODAY	SOMETHING I ENJOYED TODAY

SOMETHING I AM GRATEFUL FOR TODAY

_____

_____

_____

_____

HOW I'M FEELING ABOUT TOMORROW

_____

_____

_____

_____

plan of the day

DATE: ....

TODAY'S SCHEDULE

06.00

07.00

08.00

09.00

10.00

11.00

12.00

13.00

14.00

15.00

16.00

17.00

18.00

19.00

20.00

21.00

22.00

23.00

PRIORITIES

DON'T FORGET...   time

NOTES

reflection

SOMETHING I FOUND STRESSFUL TODAY

SOMETHING I ENJOYED TODAY

SOMETHING I AM GRATEFUL FOR TODAY

HOW I'M FEELING ABOUT TOMORROW

plan of the day

DATE: ....

TODAY'S SCHEDULE

06.00

07.00

08.00

09.00

10.00

11.00

12.00

13.00

14.00

15.00

16.00

17.00

18.00

19.00

20.00

21.00

22.00

23.00

PRIORITIES

DON'T FORGET...   time

NOTES

reflection

SOMETHING I FOUND STRESSFUL TODAY	SOMETHING I ENJOYED TODAY

SOMETHING I AM GRATEFUL FOR TODAY

HOW I'M FEELING ABOUT TOMORROW

plan of the day

DATE: ....

TODAY'S SCHEDULE

06.00

07.00

08.00

09.00

10.00

11.00

12.00

13.00

14.00

15.00

16.00

17.00

18.00

19.00

20.00

21.00

22.00

23.00

PRIORITIES

DON'T FORGET...   time

NOTES

reflection

SOMETHING I FOUND
STRESSFUL TODAY

SOMETHING I
ENJOYED TODAY

SOMETHING I AM GRATEFUL FOR TODAY

HOW I'M FEELING ABOUT TOMORROW

plan of the day

DATE: ....

TODAY'S SCHEDULE

06.00
07.00
08.00
09.00
10.00
11.00
12.00
13.00
14.00
15.00
16.00
17.00
18.00
19.00
20.00
21.00
22.00
23.00

PRIORITIES

DON'T FORGET...   time

NOTES

reflection

SOMETHING I FOUND STRESSFUL TODAY

_____

_____

_____

_____

_____

_____

_____

SOMETHING I ENJOYED TODAY

_____

_____

_____

_____

_____

_____

_____

SOMETHING I AM GRATEFUL FOR TODAY

_____

_____

_____

HOW I'M FEELING ABOUT TOMORROW

_____

_____

_____

_____

plan of the day

DATE: ....

TODAY'S SCHEDULE

06.00

07.00

08.00

09.00

10.00

11.00

12.00

13.00

14.00

15.00

16.00

17.00

18.00

19.00

20.00

21.00

22.00

23.00

PRIORITIES

DON'T FORGET...   time

NOTES

reflection

**SOMETHING I FOUND
STRESSFUL TODAY**

**SOMETHING I
ENJOYED TODAY**

SOMETHING I AM GRATEFUL FOR TODAY

HOW I'M FEELING ABOUT TOMORROW

plan of the day

DATE: ....

TODAY'S SCHEDULE

06.00
07.00
08.00
09.00
10.00
11.00
12.00
13.00
14.00
15.00
16.00
17.00
18.00
19.00
20.00
21.00
22.00
23.00

PRIORITIES

DON'T FORGET...   time

NOTES

reflection

SOMETHING I FOUND
STRESSFUL TODAY

_____

_____

_____

_____

_____

_____

_____

SOMETHING I
ENJOYED TODAY

_____

_____

_____

_____

_____

_____

_____

SOMETHING I AM GRATEFUL FOR TODAY

_____

_____

_____

_____

HOW I'M FEELING ABOUT TOMORROW

_____

_____

_____

_____

plan of the day

DATE: ....

TODAY'S SCHEDULE

06.00 _____
07.00 _____
08.00 _____
09.00 _____
10.00 _____
11.00 _____
12.00 _____
13.00 _____
14.00 _____
15.00 _____
16.00 _____
17.00 _____
18.00 _____
19.00 _____
20.00 _____
21.00 _____
22.00 _____
23.00 _____

PRIORITIES

_____
_____
_____
_____

DON'T FORGET...   time

_____   _____
_____   _____
_____   _____
_____   _____
_____   _____
_____   _____

NOTES

_____
_____
_____
_____
_____

reflection

SOMETHING I FOUND STRESSFUL TODAY	SOMETHING I ENJOYED TODAY

SOMETHING I AM GRATEFUL FOR TODAY

_____

_____

_____

_____

HOW I'M FEELING ABOUT TOMORROW

_____

_____

_____

_____

plan of the day

DATE: ....

TODAY'S SCHEDULE

06.00 _____

07.00 _____

08.00 _____

09.00 _____

10.00 _____

11.00 _____

12.00 _____

13.00 _____

14.00 _____

15.00 _____

16.00 _____

17.00 _____

18.00 _____

19.00 _____

20.00 _____

21.00 _____

22.00 _____

23.00 _____

PRIORITIES

_____

_____

_____

DON'T FORGET...   time

_____ _____

_____ _____

_____ _____

_____ _____

_____ _____

NOTES

_____

_____

_____

_____

_____

_____

reflection

SOMETHING I FOUND STRESSFUL TODAY	SOMETHING I ENJOYED TODAY

SOMETHING I AM GRATEFUL FOR TODAY

HOW I'M FEELING ABOUT TOMORROW

plan of the day

DATE: ....

TODAY'S SCHEDULE

06.00

07.00

08.00

09.00

10.00

11.00

12.00

13.00

14.00

15.00

16.00

17.00

18.00

19.00

20.00

21.00

22.00

23.00

PRIORITIES

DON'T FORGET...   time

NOTES

reflection

SOMETHING I FOUND STRESSFUL TODAY	SOMETHING I ENJOYED TODAY

SOMETHING I AM GRATEFUL FOR TODAY

HOW I'M FEELING ABOUT TOMORROW

plan of the day

DATE: ....

TODAY'S SCHEDULE

06.00 _____

07.00 _____

08.00 _____

09.00 _____

10.00 _____

11.00 _____

12.00 _____

13.00 _____

14.00 _____

15.00 _____

16.00 _____

17.00 _____

18.00 _____

19.00 _____

20.00 _____

21.00 _____

22.00 _____

23.00 _____

PRIORITIES

_____

_____

_____

DON'T FORGET...   time

_____ _____

_____ _____

_____ _____

_____ _____

_____ _____

NOTES

_____

_____

_____

_____

_____

reflection

SOMETHING I FOUND
STRESSFUL TODAY

SOMETHING I
ENJOYED TODAY

SOMETHING I AM GRATEFUL FOR TODAY

HOW I'M FEELING ABOUT TOMORROW

plan of the day

DATE: ....

TODAY'S SCHEDULE

06.00 _____

07.00 _____

08.00 _____

09.00 _____

10.00 _____

11.00 _____

12.00 _____

13.00 _____

14.00 _____

15.00 _____

16.00 _____

17.00 _____

18.00 _____

19.00 _____

20.00 _____

21.00 _____

22.00 _____

23.00 _____

PRIORITIES

DON'T FORGET...   time

NOTES

reflection

SOMETHING I FOUND STRESSFUL TODAY

SOMETHING I ENJOYED TODAY

SOMETHING I AM GRATEFUL FOR TODAY

HOW I'M FEELING ABOUT TOMORROW

---

plan of the day

DATE: ....

TODAY'S SCHEDULE

06.00 _____

07.00 _____

08.00 _____

09.00 _____

10.00 _____

11.00 _____

12.00 _____

13.00 _____

14.00 _____

15.00 _____

16.00 _____

17.00 _____

18.00 _____

19.00 _____

20.00 _____

21.00 _____

22.00 _____

23.00 _____

PRIORITIES

_____

_____

_____

DON'T FORGET...   time

_____   _____

_____   _____

_____   _____

_____   _____

_____   _____

_____   _____

NOTES

_____

_____

_____

_____

_____

_____

reflection

SOMETHING I FOUND
STRESSFUL TODAY

SOMETHING I
ENJOYED TODAY

SOMETHING I AM GRATEFUL FOR TODAY

HOW I'M FEELING ABOUT TOMORROW

plan of the day

DATE: ....

TODAY'S SCHEDULE

06.00 ....

07.00 ....

08.00 ....

09.00 ....

10.00 ....

11.00 ....

12.00 ....

13.00 ....

14.00 ....

15.00 ....

16.00 ....

17.00 ....

18.00 ....

19.00 ....

20.00 ....

21.00 ....

22.00 ....

23.00 ....

PRIORITIES

DON'T FORGET...   time

NOTES

reflection

SOMETHING I FOUND
STRESSFUL TODAY

SOMETHING I
ENJOYED TODAY

SOMETHING I AM GRATEFUL FOR TODAY

HOW I'M FEELING ABOUT TOMORROW

plan of the day

DATE: ....

TODAY'S SCHEDULE

06.00 _____

07.00 _____

08.00 _____

09.00 _____

10.00 _____

11.00 _____

12.00 _____

13.00 _____

14.00 _____

15.00 _____

16.00 _____

17.00 _____

18.00 _____

19.00 _____

20.00 _____

21.00 _____

22.00 _____

23.00 _____

PRIORITIES

_____

_____

_____

DON'T FORGET...   time

_____   _____

_____   _____

_____   _____

_____   _____

_____   _____

_____   _____

NOTES

_____

_____

_____

_____

_____

_____

reflection

SOMETHING I FOUND
STRESSFUL TODAY

SOMETHING I
ENJOYED TODAY

SOMETHING I AM GRATEFUL FOR TODAY

HOW I'M FEELING ABOUT TOMORROW

plan of the day

DATE: ....

TODAY'S SCHEDULE

06.00 _____
07.00 _____
08.00 _____
09.00 _____
10.00 _____
11.00 _____
12.00 _____
13.00 _____
14.00 _____
15.00 _____
16.00 _____
17.00 _____
18.00 _____
19.00 _____
20.00 _____
21.00 _____
22.00 _____
23.00 _____

PRIORITIES

_____
_____
_____

DON'T FORGET...   time

_____   _____
_____   _____
_____   _____
_____   _____

NOTES

_____
_____
_____
_____
_____

reflection

SOMETHING I FOUND STRESSFUL TODAY

_____
_____
_____
_____
_____
_____
_____

SOMETHING I ENJOYED TODAY

_____
_____
_____
_____
_____
_____
_____

SOMETHING I AM GRATEFUL FOR TODAY

_____
_____
_____
_____

HOW I'M FEELING ABOUT TOMORROW

_____
_____
_____
_____

plan of the day

DATE: ....

TODAY'S SCHEDULE

06.00

07.00

08.00

09.00

10.00

11.00

12.00

13.00

14.00

15.00

16.00

17.00

18.00

19.00

20.00

21.00

22.00

23.00

PRIORITIES

DON'T FORGET...   time

NOTES

reflection

SOMETHING I FOUND STRESSFUL TODAY	SOMETHING I ENJOYED TODAY

SOMETHING I AM GRATEFUL FOR TODAY

HOW I'M FEELING ABOUT TOMORROW

plan of the day

DATE: ....

TODAY'S SCHEDULE

06.00 _____

07.00 _____

08.00 _____

09.00 _____

10.00 _____

11.00 _____

12.00 _____

13.00 _____

14.00 _____

15.00 _____

16.00 _____

17.00 _____

18.00 _____

19.00 _____

20.00 _____

21.00 _____

22.00 _____

23.00 _____

PRIORITIES

_____

_____

_____

DON'T FORGET...   time

_____   _____

_____   _____

_____   _____

_____   _____

_____   _____

NOTES

_____

_____

_____

_____

_____

reflection

**SOMETHING I FOUND
STRESSFUL TODAY**

**SOMETHING I
ENJOYED TODAY**

SOMETHING I AM GRATEFUL FOR TODAY

HOW I'M FEELING ABOUT TOMORROW

plan of the day

DATE: ....

TODAY'S SCHEDULE

06.00
07.00
08.00
09.00
10.00
11.00
12.00
13.00
14.00
15.00
16.00
17.00
18.00
19.00
20.00
21.00
22.00
23.00

PRIORITIES

DON'T FORGET...   time

NOTES

reflection

**SOMETHING I FOUND
STRESSFUL TODAY**

_____

_____

_____

_____

_____

_____

_____

**SOMETHING I
ENJOYED TODAY**

_____

_____

_____

_____

_____

_____

_____

_____

SOMETHING I AM GRATEFUL FOR TODAY

_____

_____

_____

_____

HOW I'M FEELING ABOUT TOMORROW

_____

_____

_____

_____

plan of the day

DATE: ....

TODAY'S SCHEDULE

06.00
07.00
08.00
09.00
10.00
11.00
12.00
13.00
14.00
15.00
16.00
17.00
18.00
19.00
20.00
21.00
22.00
23.00

PRIORITIES

DON'T FORGET...   time

NOTES

reflection

SOMETHING I FOUND STRESSFUL TODAY

_____

_____

_____

_____

_____

_____

SOMETHING I ENJOYED TODAY

_____

_____

_____

_____

_____

_____

_____

SOMETHING I AM GRATEFUL FOR TODAY

_____

_____

_____

_____

HOW I'M FEELING ABOUT TOMORROW

_____

_____

_____

_____

plan of the day

DATE: ....

TODAY'S SCHEDULE

06.00

07.00

08.00

09.00

10.00

11.00

12.00

13.00

14.00

15.00

16.00

17.00

18.00

19.00

20.00

21.00

22.00

23.00

PRIORITIES

DON'T FORGET...   time

NOTES

reflection

**SOMETHING I FOUND
STRESSFUL TODAY**

**SOMETHING I
ENJOYED TODAY**

SOMETHING I AM GRATEFUL FOR TODAY

HOW I'M FEELING ABOUT TOMORROW

plan of the day

DATE: ....

TODAY'S SCHEDULE

06.00 _____

07.00 _____

08.00 _____

09.00 _____

10.00 _____

11.00 _____

12.00 _____

13.00 _____

14.00 _____

15.00 _____

16.00 _____

17.00 _____

18.00 _____

19.00 _____

20.00 _____

21.00 _____

22.00 _____

23.00 _____

PRIORITIES

DON'T FORGET...   time

NOTES

reflection

SOMETHING I FOUND STRESSFUL TODAY	SOMETHING I ENJOYED TODAY

SOMETHING I AM GRATEFUL FOR TODAY

HOW I'M FEELING ABOUT TOMORROW

plan of the day

DATE: ....

TODAY'S SCHEDULE

06.00 _____

07.00 _____

08.00 _____

09.00 _____

10.00 _____

11.00 _____

12.00 _____

13.00 _____

14.00 _____

15.00 _____

16.00 _____

17.00 _____

18.00 _____

19.00 _____

20.00 _____

21.00 _____

22.00 _____

23.00 _____

PRIORITIES

_____

_____

_____

DON'T FORGET...   time

_____ _____

_____ _____

_____ _____

_____ _____

_____ _____

NOTES

_____

_____

_____

_____

_____

reflection

SOMETHING I FOUND
STRESSFUL TODAY

SOMETHING I
ENJOYED TODAY

SOMETHING I AM GRATEFUL FOR TODAY

HOW I'M FEELING ABOUT TOMORROW

plan of the day

DATE: ....

TODAY'S SCHEDULE

06.00

07.00

08.00

09.00

10.00

11.00

12.00

13.00

14.00

15.00

16.00

17.00

18.00

19.00

20.00

21.00

22.00

23.00

PRIORITIES

DON'T FORGET...   time

NOTES

reflection

SOMETHING I FOUND
STRESSFUL TODAY

_____

_____

_____

_____

_____

_____

_____

SOMETHING I
ENJOYED TODAY

_____

_____

_____

_____

_____

_____

_____

SOMETHING I AM GRATEFUL FOR TODAY

_____

_____

_____

_____

HOW I'M FEELING ABOUT TOMORROW

_____

_____

_____

_____

plan of the day

DATE: ....

TODAY'S SCHEDULE

06.00 _____

07.00 _____

08.00 _____

09.00 _____

10.00 _____

11.00 _____

12.00 _____

13.00 _____

14.00 _____

15.00 _____

16.00 _____

17.00 _____

18.00 _____

19.00 _____

20.00 _____

21.00 _____

22.00 _____

23.00 _____

PRIORITIES

_____

_____

_____

DON'T FORGET...   time

_____   _____

_____   _____

_____   _____

_____   _____

_____   _____

_____   _____

NOTES

_____

_____

_____

_____

_____

reflection

SOMETHING I FOUND STRESSFUL TODAY

_____

_____

_____

_____

_____

_____

_____

SOMETHING I ENJOYED TODAY

_____

_____

_____

_____

_____

_____

_____

SOMETHING I AM GRATEFUL FOR TODAY

_____

_____

_____

_____

HOW I'M FEELING ABOUT TOMORROW

_____

_____

_____

_____

plan of the day

DATE: ....

TODAY'S SCHEDULE

06.00 _____

07.00 _____

08.00 _____

09.00 _____

10.00 _____

11.00 _____

12.00 _____

13.00 _____

14.00 _____

15.00 _____

16.00 _____

17.00 _____

18.00 _____

19.00 _____

20.00 _____

21.00 _____

22.00 _____

23.00 _____

PRIORITIES

_____

_____

_____

DON'T FORGET...   time

_____   _____

_____   _____

_____   _____

_____   _____

_____   _____

NOTES

_____

_____

_____

_____

_____

reflection

SOMETHING I FOUND STRESSFUL TODAY

_____

_____

_____

_____

_____

_____

_____

SOMETHING I ENJOYED TODAY

_____

_____

_____

_____

_____

_____

_____

SOMETHING I AM GRATEFUL FOR TODAY

_____

_____

_____

_____

HOW I'M FEELING ABOUT TOMORROW

_____

_____

_____

_____

plan of the day

DATE: ....

TODAY'S SCHEDULE

06.00 _____

07.00 _____

08.00 _____

09.00 _____

10.00 _____

11.00 _____

12.00 _____

13.00 _____

14.00 _____

15.00 _____

16.00 _____

17.00 _____

18.00 _____

19.00 _____

20.00 _____

21.00 _____

22.00 _____

23.00 _____

PRIORITIES

_____

_____

_____

DON'T FORGET...   time

_____ _____

_____ _____

_____ _____

_____ _____

_____ _____

_____ _____

NOTES

_____

_____

_____

_____

_____

reflection

**SOMETHING I FOUND
STRESSFUL TODAY**

_____

_____

_____

_____

_____

_____

**SOMETHING I
ENJOYED TODAY**

_____

_____

_____

_____

_____

_____

_____

SOMETHING I AM GRATEFUL FOR TODAY

_____

_____

_____

_____

HOW I'M FEELING ABOUT TOMORROW

_____

_____

_____

_____

plan of the day

DATE: ....

TODAY'S SCHEDULE

06.00 _____

07.00 _____

08.00 _____

09.00 _____

10.00 _____

11.00 _____

12.00 _____

13.00 _____

14.00 _____

15.00 _____

16.00 _____

17.00 _____

18.00 _____

19.00 _____

20.00 _____

21.00 _____

22.00 _____

23.00 _____

PRIORITIES

_____

_____

_____

DON'T FORGET...   time

_____ _____

_____ _____

_____ _____

_____ _____

_____ _____

_____ _____

NOTES

_____

_____

_____

_____

_____

reflection

SOMETHING I FOUND STRESSFUL TODAY

_____
_____
_____
_____
_____
_____
_____

SOMETHING I ENJOYED TODAY

_____
_____
_____
_____
_____
_____
_____

SOMETHING I AM GRATEFUL FOR TODAY

_____
_____
_____

HOW I'M FEELING ABOUT TOMORROW

_____
_____
_____
_____

plan of the day

DATE: ....

TODAY'S SCHEDULE

06.00

07.00

08.00

09.00

10.00

11.00

12.00

13.00

14.00

15.00

16.00

17.00

18.00

19.00

20.00

21.00

22.00

23.00

PRIORITIES

DON'T FORGET...   time

NOTES

reflection

SOMETHING I FOUND STRESSFUL TODAY	SOMETHING I ENJOYED TODAY

SOMETHING I AM GRATEFUL FOR TODAY

HOW I'M FEELING ABOUT TOMORROW

plan of the day

DATE: ....

TODAY'S SCHEDULE

06.00 _____
07.00 _____
08.00 _____
09.00 _____
10.00 _____
11.00 _____
12.00 _____
13.00 _____
14.00 _____
15.00 _____
16.00 _____
17.00 _____
18.00 _____
19.00 _____
20.00 _____
21.00 _____
22.00 _____
23.00 _____

PRIORITIES

_____
_____
_____

DON'T FORGET...   time

_____ _____
_____ _____
_____ _____
_____ _____
_____ _____
_____ _____

NOTES

_____
_____
_____
_____
_____

reflection

SOMETHING I FOUND
STRESSFUL TODAY

SOMETHING I
ENJOYED TODAY

SOMETHING I AM GRATEFUL FOR TODAY

HOW I'M FEELING ABOUT TOMORROW

plan of the day

DATE: ....

TODAY'S SCHEDULE

06.00 _____

07.00 _____

08.00 _____

09.00 _____

10.00 _____

11.00 _____

12.00 _____

13.00 _____

14.00 _____

15.00 _____

16.00 _____

17.00 _____

18.00 _____

19.00 _____

20.00 _____

21.00 _____

22.00 _____

23.00 _____

PRIORITIES

_____

_____

_____

DON'T FORGET...   time

_____   _____

_____   _____

_____   _____

_____   _____

_____   _____

NOTES

_____

_____

_____

_____

_____

reflection

SOMETHING I FOUND
STRESSFUL TODAY

_____

_____

_____

_____

_____

_____

_____

SOMETHING I
ENJOYED TODAY

_____

_____

_____

_____

_____

_____

_____

SOMETHING I AM GRATEFUL FOR TODAY

_____

_____

_____

_____

HOW I'M FEELING ABOUT TOMORROW

_____

_____

_____

_____

plan of the day

DATE: ....

TODAY'S SCHEDULE

06.00 _____

07.00 _____

08.00 _____

09.00 _____

10.00 _____

11.00 _____

12.00 _____

13.00 _____

14.00 _____

15.00 _____

16.00 _____

17.00 _____

18.00 _____

19.00 _____

20.00 _____

21.00 _____

22.00 _____

23.00 _____

PRIORITIES

_____

_____

_____

DON'T FORGET...   time

_____ _____

_____ _____

_____ _____

_____ _____

_____ _____

_____ _____

NOTES

_____

_____

_____

_____

_____

reflection

SOMETHING I FOUND STRESSFUL TODAY	SOMETHING I ENJOYED TODAY

SOMETHING I AM GRATEFUL FOR TODAY

HOW I'M FEELING ABOUT TOMORROW

plan of the day

DATE: ....

TODAY'S SCHEDULE

06.00 _____

07.00 _____

08.00 _____

09.00 _____

10.00 _____

11.00 _____

12.00 _____

13.00 _____

14.00 _____

15.00 _____

16.00 _____

17.00 _____

18.00 _____

19.00 _____

20.00 _____

21.00 _____

22.00 _____

23.00 _____

PRIORITIES

_____

_____

_____

DON'T FORGET...   time

_____   _____

_____   _____

_____   _____

_____   _____

_____   _____

NOTES

_____

_____

_____

_____

_____

reflection

SOMETHING I FOUND STRESSFUL TODAY

SOMETHING I ENJOYED TODAY

SOMETHING I AM GRATEFUL FOR TODAY

HOW I'M FEELING ABOUT TOMORROW

DATE: ....

TODAY'S SCHEDULE

06.00 _____

07.00 _____

08.00 _____

09.00 _____

10.00 _____

11.00 _____

12.00 _____

13.00 _____

14.00 _____

15.00 _____

16.00 _____

17.00 _____

18.00 _____

19.00 _____

20.00 _____

21.00 _____

22.00 _____

23.00 _____

PRIORITIES

_____

_____

_____

DON'T FORGET...   time

_____ _____

_____ _____

_____ _____

_____ _____

_____ _____

_____ _____

NOTES

_____

_____

_____

_____

_____

reflection

SOMETHING I FOUND
STRESSFUL TODAY

SOMETHING I
ENJOYED TODAY

SOMETHING I AM GRATEFUL FOR TODAY

HOW I'M FEELING ABOUT TOMORROW

plan of the day

DATE: ....

TODAY'S SCHEDULE

06.00 _____

07.00 _____

08.00 _____

09.00 _____

10.00 _____

11.00 _____

12.00 _____

13.00 _____

14.00 _____

15.00 _____

16.00 _____

17.00 _____

18.00 _____

19.00 _____

20.00 _____

21.00 _____

22.00 _____

23.00 _____

PRIORITIES

_____

_____

_____

DON'T FORGET...   time

_____ _____

_____ _____

_____ _____

_____ _____

_____ _____

NOTES

_____

_____

_____

_____

_____

reflection

SOMETHING I FOUND STRESSFUL TODAY	SOMETHING I ENJOYED TODAY

SOMETHING I AM GRATEFUL FOR TODAY

HOW I'M FEELING ABOUT TOMORROW

plan of the day

DATE: ....

TODAY'S SCHEDULE

06.00 _____

07.00 _____

08.00 _____

09.00 _____

10.00 _____

11.00 _____

12.00 _____

13.00 _____

14.00 _____

15.00 _____

16.00 _____

17.00 _____

18.00 _____

19.00 _____

20.00 _____

21.00 _____

22.00 _____

23.00 _____

PRIORITIES

_____

_____

_____

DON'T FORGET...   time

_____   _____

_____   _____

_____   _____

_____   _____

_____   _____

NOTES

_____

_____

_____

_____

_____

reflection

SOMETHING I FOUND
STRESSFUL TODAY

_____

_____

_____

_____

_____

_____

_____

SOMETHING I
ENJOYED TODAY

_____

_____

_____

_____

_____

_____

_____

SOMETHING I AM GRATEFUL FOR TODAY

_____

_____

_____

_____

HOW I'M FEELING ABOUT TOMORROW

_____

_____

_____

_____

plan of the day

DATE: ....

TODAY'S SCHEDULE

06.00 _____

07.00 _____

08.00 _____

09.00 _____

10.00 _____

11.00 _____

12.00 _____

13.00 _____

14.00 _____

15.00 _____

16.00 _____

17.00 _____

18.00 _____

19.00 _____

20.00 _____

21.00 _____

22.00 _____

23.00 _____

PRIORITIES

_____
_____
_____

DON'T FORGET...   time

_____ ____

_____ ____

_____ ____

_____ ____

_____ ____

_____ ____

NOTES

_____
_____
_____
_____
_____
_____

reflection

SOMETHING I FOUND
STRESSFUL TODAY

SOMETHING I
ENJOYED TODAY

SOMETHING I AM GRATEFUL FOR TODAY

HOW I'M FEELING ABOUT TOMORROW

plan of the day

DATE: ....

TODAY'S SCHEDULE

06.00

07.00

08.00

09.00

10.00

11.00

12.00

13.00

14.00

15.00

16.00

17.00

18.00

19.00

20.00

21.00

22.00

23.00

PRIORITIES

DON'T FORGET...   time

NOTES

reflection

**SOMETHING I FOUND
STRESSFUL TODAY**

**SOMETHING I
ENJOYED TODAY**

SOMETHING I AM GRATEFUL FOR TODAY

HOW I'M FEELING ABOUT TOMORROW

plan of the day

DATE: ....

TODAY'S SCHEDULE

06.00 _____
07.00 _____
08.00 _____
09.00 _____
10.00 _____
11.00 _____
12.00 _____
13.00 _____
14.00 _____
15.00 _____
16.00 _____
17.00 _____
18.00 _____
19.00 _____
20.00 _____
21.00 _____
22.00 _____
23.00 _____

PRIORITIES

DON'T FORGET...   time

NOTES

reflection

SOMETHING I FOUND
STRESSFUL TODAY

_____

_____

_____

_____

_____

_____

_____

SOMETHING I
ENJOYED TODAY

_____

_____

_____

_____

_____

_____

_____

_____

SOMETHING I AM GRATEFUL FOR TODAY

_____

_____

_____

_____

HOW I'M FEELING ABOUT TOMORROW

_____

_____

_____

_____

plan of the day

DATE: ....

TODAY'S SCHEDULE

06.00 _____

07.00 _____

08.00 _____

09.00 _____

10.00 _____

11.00 _____

12.00 _____

13.00 _____

14.00 _____

15.00 _____

16.00 _____

17.00 _____

18.00 _____

19.00 _____

20.00 _____

21.00 _____

22.00 _____

23.00 _____

PRIORITIES

_____

_____

_____

DON'T FORGET...   time

_____ _____

_____ _____

_____ _____

_____ _____

_____ _____

NOTES

_____

_____

_____

_____

_____

reflection

SOMETHING I FOUND STRESSFUL TODAY	SOMETHING I ENJOYED TODAY

SOMETHING I AM GRATEFUL FOR TODAY

HOW I'M FEELING ABOUT TOMORROW

plan of the day

DATE: ....

TODAY'S SCHEDULE

06.00 _____

07.00 _____

08.00 _____

09.00 _____

10.00 _____

11.00 _____

12.00 _____

13.00 _____

14.00 _____

15.00 _____

16.00 _____

17.00 _____

18.00 _____

19.00 _____

20.00 _____

21.00 _____

22.00 _____

23.00 _____

PRIORITIES

_____

_____

_____

DON'T FORGET...   time

_____ _____

_____ _____

_____ _____

_____ _____

_____ _____

NOTES

_____

_____

_____

_____

_____

reflection

SOMETHING I FOUND STRESSFUL TODAY	SOMETHING I ENJOYED TODAY

SOMETHING I AM GRATEFUL FOR TODAY

HOW I'M FEELING ABOUT TOMORROW

plan of the day

DATE: ....

TODAY'S SCHEDULE

06.00 _____

07.00 _____

08.00 _____

09.00 _____

10.00 _____

11.00 _____

12.00 _____

13.00 _____

14.00 _____

15.00 _____

16.00 _____

17.00 _____

18.00 _____

19.00 _____

20.00 _____

21.00 _____

22.00 _____

23.00 _____

PRIORITIES

_____

_____

_____

_____

DON'T FORGET...   time

_____   _____

_____   _____

_____   _____

_____   _____

_____   _____

NOTES

_____

_____

_____

_____

_____

reflection

SOMETHING I FOUND STRESSFUL TODAY	SOMETHING I ENJOYED TODAY

SOMETHING I AM GRATEFUL FOR TODAY

HOW I'M FEELING ABOUT TOMORROW

plan of the day

DATE: ....

TODAY'S SCHEDULE

06.00 _____
07.00 _____
08.00 _____
09.00 _____
10.00 _____
11.00 _____
12.00 _____
13.00 _____
14.00 _____
15.00 _____
16.00 _____
17.00 _____
18.00 _____
19.00 _____
20.00 _____
21.00 _____
22.00 _____
23.00 _____

PRIORITIES
_____
_____
_____

DON'T FORGET...   time
_____ _____
_____ _____
_____ _____
_____ _____
_____ _____
_____ _____

NOTES
_____
_____
_____
_____
_____

reflection

SOMETHING I FOUND
STRESSFUL TODAY

SOMETHING I
ENJOYED TODAY

SOMETHING I AM GRATEFUL FOR TODAY

HOW I'M FEELING ABOUT TOMORROW

plan of the day

DATE: ....

TODAY'S SCHEDULE

06.00 _____

07.00 _____

08.00 _____

09.00 _____

10.00 _____

11.00 _____

12.00 _____

13.00 _____

14.00 _____

15.00 _____

16.00 _____

17.00 _____

18.00 _____

19.00 _____

20.00 _____

21.00 _____

22.00 _____

23.00 _____

PRIORITIES

_____

_____

_____

DON'T FORGET...   time

_____   _____

_____   _____

_____   _____

_____   _____

_____   _____

_____   _____

NOTES

_____

_____

_____

_____

_____

reflection

SOMETHING I FOUND STRESSFUL TODAY	SOMETHING I ENJOYED TODAY

SOMETHING I AM GRATEFUL FOR TODAY

HOW I'M FEELING ABOUT TOMORROW

plan of the day

DATE: ....

TODAY'S SCHEDULE

06.00 _____

07.00 _____

08.00 _____

09.00 _____

10.00 _____

11.00 _____

12.00 _____

13.00 _____

14.00 _____

15.00 _____

16.00 _____

17.00 _____

18.00 _____

19.00 _____

20.00 _____

21.00 _____

22.00 _____

23.00 _____

PRIORITIES

_____

_____

_____

DON'T FORGET...   time

_____ _____

_____ _____

_____ _____

_____ _____

_____ _____

_____ _____

NOTES

_____

_____

_____

_____

_____

reflection

SOMETHING I FOUND
STRESSFUL TODAY

_____

_____

_____

_____

_____

_____

SOMETHING I
ENJOYED TODAY

_____

_____

_____

_____

_____

_____

_____

SOMETHING I AM GRATEFUL FOR TODAY

_____

_____

_____

_____

HOW I'M FEELING ABOUT TOMORROW

_____

_____

_____

_____

plan of the day

DATE: ....

TODAY'S SCHEDULE

06.00

07.00

08.00

09.00

10.00

11.00

12.00

13.00

14.00

15.00

16.00

17.00

18.00

19.00

20.00

21.00

22.00

23.00

PRIORITIES

DON'T FORGET...   time

NOTES

reflection

SOMETHING I FOUND STRESSFUL TODAY	SOMETHING I ENJOYED TODAY

SOMETHING I AM GRATEFUL FOR TODAY

HOW I'M FEELING ABOUT TOMORROW

plan of the day

DATE: ....

TODAY'S SCHEDULE

06.00 _____
07.00 _____
08.00 _____
09.00 _____
10.00 _____
11.00 _____
12.00 _____
13.00 _____
14.00 _____
15.00 _____
16.00 _____
17.00 _____
18.00 _____
19.00 _____
20.00 _____
21.00 _____
22.00 _____
23.00 _____

PRIORITIES

_____
_____
_____

DON'T FORGET...   time

_____ _____
_____ _____
_____ _____
_____ _____
_____ _____
_____ _____

NOTES

_____
_____
_____
_____
_____
_____

SOMETHING I FOUND STRESSFUL TODAY	SOMETHING I ENJOYED TODAY

SOMETHING I AM GRATEFUL FOR TODAY

HOW I'M FEELING ABOUT TOMORROW

plan of the day

DATE: ....

TODAY'S SCHEDULE

06.00 _____
07.00 _____
08.00 _____
09.00 _____
10.00 _____
11.00 _____
12.00 _____
13.00 _____
14.00 _____
15.00 _____
16.00 _____
17.00 _____
18.00 _____
19.00 _____
20.00 _____
21.00 _____
22.00 _____
23.00 _____

PRIORITIES

DON'T FORGET...   time

NOTES

reflection

SOMETHING I FOUND STRESSFUL TODAY	SOMETHING I ENJOYED TODAY

SOMETHING I AM GRATEFUL FOR TODAY

HOW I'M FEELING ABOUT TOMORROW

plan of the day

DATE: ....

TODAY'S SCHEDULE

06.00 _____

07.00 _____

08.00 _____

09.00 _____

10.00 _____

11.00 _____

12.00 _____

13.00 _____

14.00 _____

15.00 _____

16.00 _____

17.00 _____

18.00 _____

19.00 _____

20.00 _____

21.00 _____

22.00 _____

23.00 _____

PRIORITIES

_____

_____

_____

DON'T FORGET...   time

_____ _____

_____ _____

_____ _____

_____ _____

_____ _____

_____ _____

NOTES

_____

_____

_____

_____

_____

_____

reflection

SOMETHING I FOUND
STRESSFUL TODAY

SOMETHING I
ENJOYED TODAY

SOMETHING I AM GRATEFUL FOR TODAY

HOW I'M FEELING ABOUT TOMORROW

plan of the day

DATE: ....

TODAY'S SCHEDULE

06.00 _____

07.00 _____

08.00 _____

09.00 _____

10.00 _____

11.00 _____

12.00 _____

13.00 _____

14.00 _____

15.00 _____

16.00 _____

17.00 _____

18.00 _____

19.00 _____

20.00 _____

21.00 _____

22.00 _____

23.00 _____

PRIORITIES

_____

_____

_____

DON'T FORGET...   time

_____ _____

_____ _____

_____ _____

_____ _____

_____ _____

NOTES

_____

_____

_____

_____

_____

reflection

SOMETHING I FOUND STRESSFUL TODAY	SOMETHING I ENJOYED TODAY

SOMETHING I AM GRATEFUL FOR TODAY

HOW I'M FEELING ABOUT TOMORROW

plan of the day

DATE: ....

TODAY'S SCHEDULE

06.00
07.00
08.00
09.00
10.00
11.00
12.00
13.00
14.00
15.00
16.00
17.00
18.00
19.00
20.00
21.00
22.00
23.00

PRIORITIES

DON'T FORGET...   time

NOTES

reflection

SOMETHING I FOUND
STRESSFUL TODAY

SOMETHING I
ENJOYED TODAY

SOMETHING I AM GRATEFUL FOR TODAY

HOW I'M FEELING ABOUT TOMORROW

---

plan of the day

DATE: ....

TODAY'S SCHEDULE

06.00
07.00
08.00
09.00
10.00
11.00
12.00
13.00
14.00
15.00
16.00
17.00
18.00
19.00
20.00
21.00
22.00
23.00

PRIORITIES

DON'T FORGET...   time

NOTES

reflection

SOMETHING I FOUND
STRESSFUL TODAY

SOMETHING I
ENJOYED TODAY

SOMETHING I AM GRATEFUL FOR TODAY

HOW I'M FEELING ABOUT TOMORROW

plan of the day

DATE: ....

TODAY'S SCHEDULE

06.00 _____

07.00 _____

08.00 _____

09.00 _____

10.00 _____

11.00 _____

12.00 _____

13.00 _____

14.00 _____

15.00 _____

16.00 _____

17.00 _____

18.00 _____

19.00 _____

20.00 _____

21.00 _____

22.00 _____

23.00 _____

PRIORITIES

_____

_____

_____

DON'T FORGET...   time

_____ _____

_____ _____

_____ _____

_____ _____

_____ _____

NOTES

_____

_____

_____

_____

_____

reflection

SOMETHING I FOUND
STRESSFUL TODAY

SOMETHING I
ENJOYED TODAY

SOMETHING I AM GRATEFUL FOR TODAY

HOW I'M FEELING ABOUT TOMORROW

plan of the day

DATE: ....

TODAY'S SCHEDULE

06.00 _____

07.00 _____

08.00 _____

09.00 _____

10.00 _____

11.00 _____

12.00 _____

13.00 _____

14.00 _____

15.00 _____

16.00 _____

17.00 _____

18.00 _____

19.00 _____

20.00 _____

21.00 _____

22.00 _____

23.00 _____

PRIORITIES

_____

_____

_____

DON'T FORGET...   time

_____ _____

_____ _____

_____ _____

_____ _____

_____ _____

_____ _____

NOTES

_____

_____

_____

_____

_____

reflection

SOMETHING I FOUND STRESSFUL TODAY	SOMETHING I ENJOYED TODAY

SOMETHING I AM GRATEFUL FOR TODAY

HOW I'M FEELING ABOUT TOMORROW

Feel Good To-do Lists

DATE: ....

- ○ _____
- ○ _____
- ○ _____
- ○ _____
- ○ _____
- ○ _____
- ○ _____
- ○ _____
- ○ _____

DATE: ....

- ○ _____
- ○ _____
- ○ _____
- ○ _____
- ○ _____
- ○ _____
- ○ _____
- ○ _____
- ○ _____

feel good to-do lists

DATE: ....

- ○ _____
- ○ _____
- ○ _____
- ○ _____
- ○ _____
- ○ _____
- ○ _____
- ○ _____
- ○ _____

DATE: ....

- ○ _____
- ○ _____
- ○ _____
- ○ _____
- ○ _____
- ○ _____
- ○ _____
- ○ _____
- ○ _____

feel good to-do lists

DATE: ....

○ _____
○ _____
○ _____
○ _____
○ _____
○ _____
○ _____
○ _____
○ _____

DATE: ....

○ _____
○ _____
○ _____
○ _____
○ _____
○ _____
○ _____
○ _____
○ _____

feel good to-do lists

DATE: ....

- ○ _____
- ○ _____
- ○ _____
- ○ _____
- ○ _____
- ○ _____
- ○ _____
- ○ _____
- ○ _____

DATE: ....

- ○ _____
- ○ _____
- ○ _____
- ○ _____
- ○ _____
- ○ _____
- ○ _____
- ○ _____
- ○ _____

PART TWO

Your Reflection Activities

Welcome to the second part of your planner, your reflection activities! This part is full of quick and simple interactive activities that I have found really helpful over the years. It amazes me how taking a small amount of time to get my thoughts down on paper through these simple activities has helped me feel so much more in control of my emotions, my motivation and my overall happiness. I hope you find these little activites as helpful as I have and enjoy them as much as I do. Let's go!

What's included

Anxiety Dump

The CBT Cycle

Reframing Negative Thoughts

Gratitude Lists

Self-care Planner

Special Memories

Seasonal Refresh

Anxiety Dump

Sometimes, when there are so many anxiety-inducing thoughts running through your head, it can feel incredibly overwhelming and it feels impossible to know what to do and where to start. I have found one of the most simple and helpful things is just sorting out all my anxious thoughts and dumping them into my anxiety dump.

WHAT'S MAKING ME FEEL ANXIOUS?

THINGS IN MY CONTROL

THINGS OUT OF MY CONTROL

SHORT TERM TO-DO LIST

LONGER TERM TO-DO LIST

HOW AM I FEELING NOW?

---

anxiety dump

DATE: ....

WHAT'S MAKING ME FEEL ANXIOUS?

_____

_____

_____

THINGS IN MY CONTROL

_____

_____

THINGS OUT OF MY CONTROL

_____

_____

SHORT TERM TO-DO LIST

_____

_____

LONGER TERM TO-DO LIST

_____

_____

HOW AM I FEELING NOW?

_____

_____

_____

anxiety dump

DATE: ....

WHAT'S MAKING ME FEEL ANXIOUS?

_____

_____

_____

THINGS IN MY CONTROL	THINGS OUT OF MY CONTROL
_____	_____
_____	_____
_____	_____

SHORT TERM TO-DO LIST	LONGER TERM TO-DO LIST
_____	_____
_____	_____
_____	_____

HOW AM I FEELING NOW?

_____

_____

_____

anxiety dump

DATE: ....

WHAT'S MAKING ME FEEL ANXIOUS?

_____

_____

_____

THINGS IN MY CONTROL

_____

_____

THINGS OUT OF MY CONTROL

_____

_____

SHORT TERM TO-DO LIST

_____

_____

LONGER TERM TO-DO LIST

_____

_____

HOW AM I FEELING NOW?

_____

_____

_____

anxiety dump

DATE: ....

WHAT'S MAKING ME FEEL ANXIOUS?

_____

_____

_____

THINGS IN MY CONTROL

_____

_____

THINGS OUT OF MY CONTROL

_____

_____

SHORT TERM TO-DO LIST

_____

_____

_____

LONGER TERM TO-DO LIST

_____

_____

_____

HOW AM I FEELING NOW?

_____

_____

_____

anxiety dump

DATE: ....

WHAT'S MAKING ME FEEL ANXIOUS?

_____

_____

_____

THINGS IN MY CONTROL

_____

_____

_____

THINGS OUT OF MY CONTROL

_____

_____

_____

SHORT TERM TO-DO LIST

_____

_____

_____

LONGER TERM TO-DO LIST

_____

_____

_____

HOW AM I FEELING NOW?

_____

_____

_____

The CBT Cycle

Cognitive Behavioural Therapy (CBT) is a well-used form of therapy for anxiety and depression. It essentially helps you to understand when you are creating negative emotions and behaviour from a thought that might not even be true! Our emotions can so easily run away from us; before we know it we've created a vicious cycle of negative thoughts that came from no actual facts but often just assumption!

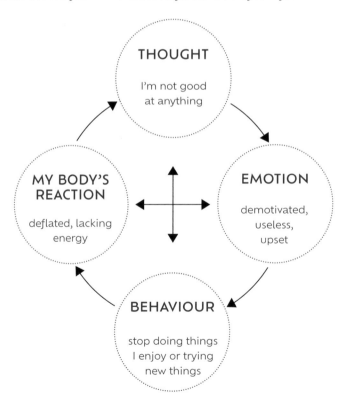

CBT is essentially a set of practices to help change negative and damaging thought patterns and feelings to enable us to cope with them better. Our internal dialogue, which often manifests as doubt and anxiety, can feel so powerful, but there are practical tools we can all learn to help improve these feelings and make us feel calmer and more in control.

Here are some practices and prompts you could try when you're feeling anxious about something:

Journalling – good news, journalling is considered an important practice within CBT, so you're already on the right track! Writing scary thoughts down can help to rationalize them and can make them feel smaller, so it's really worth doing if they're taking up a lot of space in your brain. I've included some 'anxiety dump' prompts to help get you started on the previous few pages, which you can come back to whenever you need to.

Breathing – there are lots of guided meditations that you can find on YouTube, online, and on apps and podcasts, here's a simple one to try:

- Get into a comfortable position, sitting, lying or standing;

- Place one hand on your chest and one hand on your tummy;

- Breathe slowly in through your nose and feel the breath flow deep down into your tummy so that you can see it expand; try to keep the hand on your chest still;

- Breathe slowly out through your mouth; pursing your lips helps to keep your breath slow and steady;

- Do this for 3 to 5 minutes, or until you feel calmer.

Muscle relaxation – find a comfortable position (lying down is best). Begin by tensing your shoulders up for a few seconds, then releasing them as you breathe out, trying to completely relax your muscles. Repeat this for each body part, while focusing on your breathing. You'll be surprised at how differently you feel afterwards!

DATE: ....

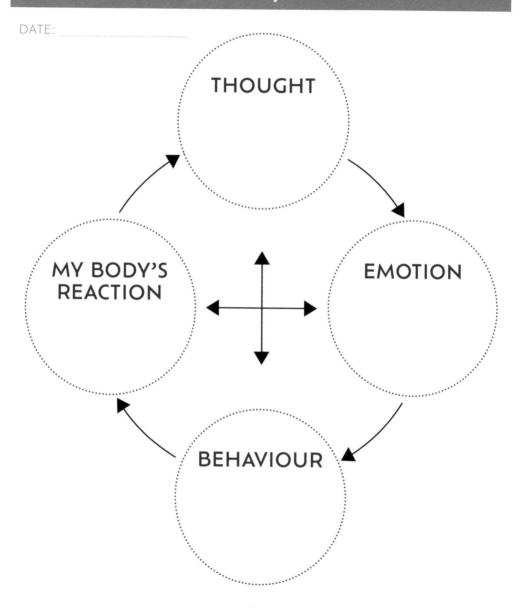

THOUGHT

MY BODY'S
REACTION

EMOTION

BEHAVIOUR

DATE: ....

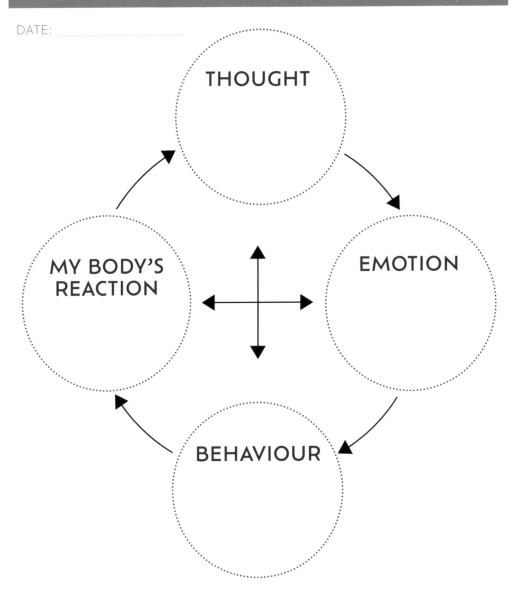

THOUGHT

MY BODY'S
REACTION

EMOTION

BEHAVIOUR

CBT cycle

DATE: ....

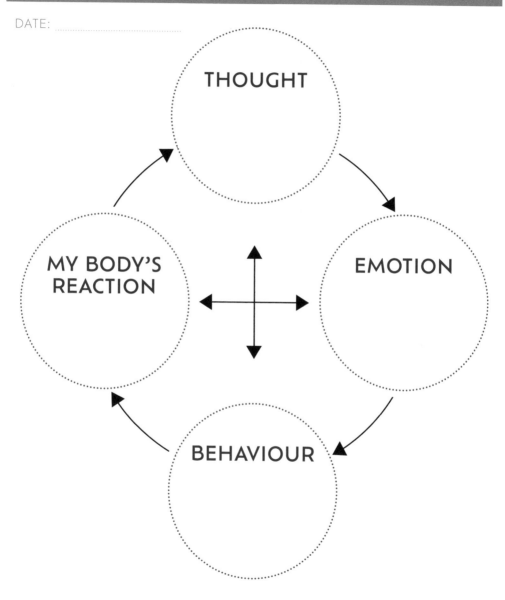

THOUGHT

MY BODY'S
REACTION

EMOTION

BEHAVIOUR

DATE: ....

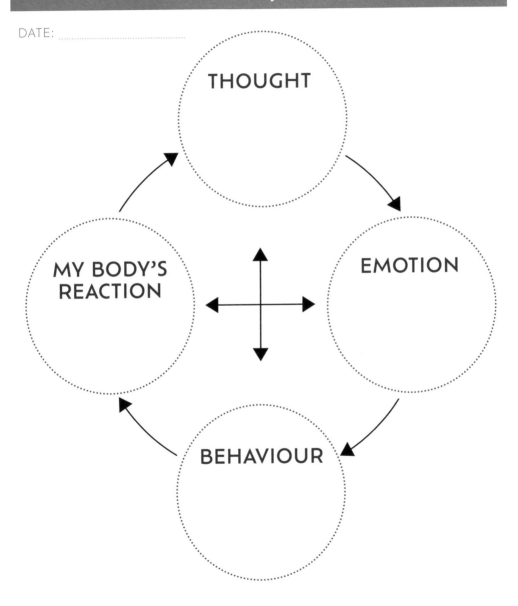

DATE: ....

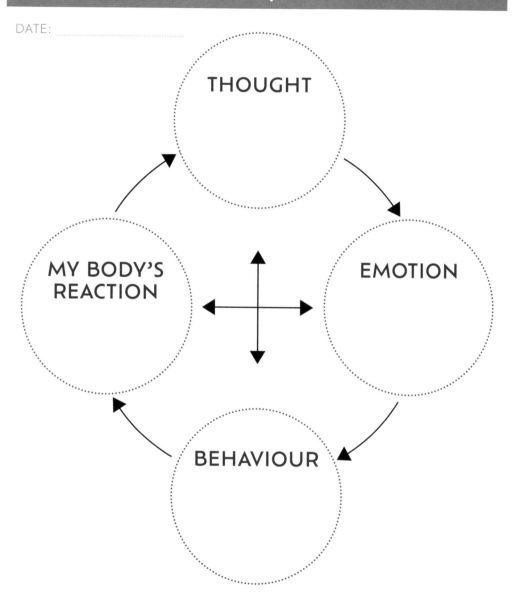

Reframing Negative Thoughts

The mind is so incredibly powerful and I am such a strong believer that the energy we give off is created by how we process our daily thoughts. I remember so vividly seeing a quote in a museum by the Roman Emperor Marcus Aurelius a few years ago that said 'The soul becomes dyed with the colour of its thoughts' and I've never forgotten it! I have always been someone that really struggles with processing my thoughts as I so easily doubt myself and create worst case scenarios in my head even without any facts to back them up!

Example:

NEGATIVE THOUGHT: I don't feel like I'm doing well enough at work/at university/in school...

POSITIVE REFRAME: I'm so proud of how far I've come. I'm proud that I want to work hard and achieve my best but all I can ask of myself is that I try my hardest.

NEGATIVE THOUGHT: I'm feeling so unfit.

POSITIVE REFRAME: Life is always changing and sometimes it gets incredibly difficult to fit any exercise/movement in! I really want to start incorporating exercise back into my weekly routine whenever possible, so I'm going to sit down and create an achievable plan for this!

DATE:

NEGATIVE THOUGHT:

_____

_____

_____

POSITIVE REFRAME:

_____

_____

_____

DATE:

NEGATIVE THOUGHT:

_____

_____

_____

POSITIVE REFRAME:

_____

_____

_____

DATE: ....

NEGATIVE THOUGHT:

_____

_____

_____

POSITIVE REFRAME:

_____

_____

_____

DATE: ....

NEGATIVE THOUGHT:

_____

_____

_____

POSITIVE REFRAME:

_____

_____

_____

reframing negative thoughts

DATE: ....

NEGATIVE THOUGHT:

_____

_____

_____

POSITIVE REFRAME:

_____

_____

_____

DATE: ....

NEGATIVE THOUGHT:

_____

_____

_____

POSITIVE REFRAME:

_____

_____

_____

reframing negative thoughts

DATE: ....

NEGATIVE THOUGHT:

_____

_____

_____

POSITIVE REFRAME:

_____

_____

_____

DATE: ....

NEGATIVE THOUGHT:

_____

_____

_____

POSITIVE REFRAME:

_____

_____

_____

Gratitude List

Just taking a few minutes to jot down some things you feel grateful for can really help create positive energy and mindset to start or end your day with!

DATE: ....

THINGS I'M FEELING GRATEFUL FOR (BIG OR SMALL)

_____

_____

_____

_____

_____

DATE: ....

THINGS I'M FEELING GRATEFUL FOR (BIG OR SMALL)

_____

_____

_____

_____

_____

gratitude list

DATE: ....

THINGS I'M FEELING GRATEFUL FOR (BIG OR SMALL)

_____

_____

_____

_____

_____

_____

DATE: ....

THINGS I'M FEELING GRATEFUL FOR (BIG OR SMALL)

_____

_____

_____

_____

_____

_____

_____

gratitude list

DATE: ....

THINGS I'M FEELING GRATEFUL FOR (BIG OR SMALL)

DATE: ....

THINGS I'M FEELING GRATEFUL FOR (BIG OR SMALL)

Self-care Day Planner Example

light a candle

I always buy myself a special candle, which signifies 'time off', so whenever I light this candle it signals to my brain that it's time to switch off and relax.

switch off technology

I find it impossible to fully relax when my phone or laptop is right next to me to be checked at any time. I try to move my devices completely out of my sight for a few hours. Out of sight, out of mind!

doing my nails

movement

If I choose movement for self care I try to think carefully about what type of movement is best going to care for my body that day and be most enjoyable. My favourites are a walk outside, a quick sweaty home workout or a slow yoga session.

journalling / reflection time

face mask or skincare routine

self-care day planner

DATE: ....

THINGS I'M GOING TO DO TODAY...

self-care day planner

DATE:

THINGS I'M GOING TO DO TODAY...

self-care day planner

DATE: ....

THINGS I'M GOING TO DO TODAY...

Special Memories

special memories

THINGS I HAVE LEARNT ABOUT MYSELF

_____
_____
_____
_____
_____
_____
_____
_____
_____
_____

THINGS I APPRECIATE AND LOVE ABOUT MYSELF

_____
_____
_____
_____
_____
_____
_____
_____
_____
_____

THINGS I HAVE LET GO OF

_____

_____

_____

_____

_____

_____

_____

_____

_____

_____

THINGS THAT MAKE ME PROUD OF MYSELF

_____

_____

_____

_____

_____

_____

_____

_____

_____

_____

_____

Stay close to
people who feel
like sunshine

Seasonal Refresh

I'm such a fan of celebrating the seasons as they change and I've found that adding a little seasonal planning into my year has really helped to keep the changing seasons exciting and motivating rather than overwhelming or daunting. Going into autumn/winter can be challenging if, like me and so many others, you find you're very sensitive to changes in daylight. The change in weather and reduced daylight around these months can affect your mood and energy levels so much. Then, as we move away from autumn/winter and into spring/summer, it can bring on an overwhelming need to 'shape up' for summer and suddenly become the 'new you'. To help with this, before each season I now try to do some seasonal planning to help keep my focus away from these negative emotions and onto more positive and motivating thoughts and ideas for the upcoming seasons.

autumn refresh

AUTUMN IDEAS TICK LIST

The idea is not to tick off every idea here but to pick and choose a selection that you'd love to plan into your upcoming months for this season.

After the tick lists for each season I've made sure to include some space to add any other exciting plans or ideas you have or any notes you want to make alongside your seasonal planning.

○ go pumpkin picking

○ decorate for autumn

○ make a DIY autumn wreath

○ bake a pumpkin pie

○ plan a movie night

○ buy an autumn candle

○ decorate with fairy lights

○ make some s'mores

○ create a luxury hot chocolate

   with marshmallows and cream

○ go on an autumn walk

○ start a new craft activity

○ start a puzzle

○ bake a comforting pie

○ plan a coffee date with a friend

○ bake cookies

○ make time for journalling

○ organise your wardrobe ready

   for the colder months

○ carve pumpkins

○ host a halloween dinner party

○ go to a bonfire night event

○ curl up with a book

○ have a PJ and fluffy socks day

○ try some at-home yoga

OTHER EXCITING PLANS/IDEAS I HAVE FOR THIS AUTUMN...

- ○ _____
- ○ _____
- ○ _____
- ○ _____
- ○ _____
- ○ _____
- ○ _____
- ○ _____

EXTRA NOTES FOR PLANNING MY IDEAS...

_____

_____

_____

_____

_____

_____

_____

_____

_____

_____

_____

WINTER IDEAS TICK LIST

The idea is not to tick off every idea here but to pick and choose a selection that you'd love to plan into your upcoming months for this season.

After the tick lists for each season I've made sure to include some space to add any other exciting plans or ideas you have or any notes you want to make alongside your seasonal planning.

○ decorate with cosy lights/candles

○ go ice skating

○ have a movie day in your PJs

○ make gingerbread biscuits

○ plan a movie night with a friend

○ buy yourself a festive candle

○ pamper night (face mask, book, wine...)

○ make a festive/winter themed grazing snack board (Pinterest it!)

○ wrap up and go on a winter walk

○ watch Christmas films

○ cook a new recipe

○ make some DIY christmas cards

○ decorate for Christmas

○ journalling/reflecting on the past year

○ plan a hot chocolate/coffee date with a friend

○ have a bubble bath

○ host a Christmas/winter dinner party

○ go to a christmas lights event

○ donate to a charity you'd love to support

○ have a pyjama day

○ winter/Christmas markets

○ decorate a gingerbread house

OTHER EXCITING PLANS/IDEAS I HAVE FOR THIS WINTER...

- ○ _____
- ○ _____
- ○ _____
- ○ _____
- ○ _____
- ○ _____
- ○ _____
- ○ _____

EXTRA NOTES FOR PLANNING MY IDEAS...

_____
_____
_____
_____
_____
_____
_____
_____
_____
_____
_____
_____

SPRING IDEAS TICK LIST

The idea is not to tick off every idea here but to pick and choose a selection that you'd love to plan into your upcoming months for this season.
After the tick lists for each season I've made sure to include some space to add any other exciting plans or ideas you have or any notes you want to make alongside your seasonal planning.

- ○ buy yourself some fresh flowers
- ○ increase water intake
- ○ plan a beach walk
- ○ make time for journalling/ mindfulness
- ○ invite friends over for a homemade meal
- ○ cook with seasonal fruit/veggies
- ○ decorate with Easter home decor
- ○ go on a bike ride
- ○ plan a social media/technology break for 24 hours
- ○ plan a picnic

- ○ buy some new fresh-smelling soaps
- ○ organise your wardrobe for upcoming warmer weather
- ○ bake something new
- ○ DIY Easter crafts (Pinterest it!)
- ○ spring clean
- ○ plant some flowers in your garden
- ○ pizza and movie night
- ○ spring walks
- ○ pamper yourself (facial, fresh nails)
- ○ plan a day trip
- ○ brunch with a friend

OTHER EXCITING PLANS/IDEAS I HAVE FOR THIS SPRING...

- ○ _____
- ○ _____
- ○ _____
- ○ _____
- ○ _____
- ○ _____
- ○ _____
- ○ _____

EXTRA NOTES FOR PLANNING MY IDEAS...

summer refresh

SUMMER IDEAS TICK LIST

The idea is not to tick off every idea here but to pick and choose a selection that you'd love to plan into your upcoming months for this season.

After the tick lists for each season I've made sure to include some space to add any other exciting plans or ideas you have or any notes you want to make alongside your seasonal planning.

- ○ strawberry picking
- ○ organise your summer clothes
- ○ make fruit-infused water
- ○ walks in the sun
- ○ have a BBQ with friends
- ○ try some yoga/meditation exercises
- ○ try a new activity or sport
- ○ fresh home decor
- ○ bike rides
- ○ plan regular social media breaks
- ○ plan a picnic with friends
- ○ go for a swim in the sea

- ○ go for a hike
- ○ try a new pasta salad recipe
- ○ go charity/thrift shopping
- ○ make homemade ice lollies
- ○ make time for journalling/ mindfulness
- ○ try a new hobby (pottery, painting...)
- ○ watch the sunset
- ○ paint your nails a colour that makes you smile
- ○ make a smoothie
- ○ plan a road trip

OTHER EXCITING PLANS/IDEAS I HAVE FOR THIS SUMMER...

- ○ _____
- ○ _____
- ○ _____
- ○ _____
- ○ _____
- ○ _____
- ○ _____
- ○ _____

EXTRA NOTES FOR PLANNING MY IDEAS...

Thank you for joining me
on this journey. I hope
you have enjoyed using
this journal and that it has
provided something you
needed it to – small or big!